KT-198-895

Meredith

Meredith

JOHN KERCHER

HODDER &
STOUGHTON

First published in Great Britain in 2012 by Hodder & Stoughton
An Hachette UK company

3

Copyright © John Kercher 2012

The right of John Kercher to be identified as the Author of the Work has been
asserted by him in accordance with the Copyright, Designs and Patents Act 1988.

Picture Acknowledgements
Courtesy of the Kercher family: pages 1–8, 9–10. © Getty Images:
pages 11 below, 14 below, 15 above. © Press Association Images:
page 16 above and centre. © Rex Features: pages 11 above, 12–13,
14 above and centre, 15 centre and below, 16 below.

All rights reserved. No part of this publication may be reproduced, stored
in a retrieval system, or transmitted, in any form or by any means without
the prior written permission of the publisher, nor be otherwise circulated in
any form of binding or cover other than that in which it is published and
without a similar condition being imposed on the subsequent purchaser.

A CIP catalogue record for this title is available from the British Library

ISBN 978 1 444 74276 3
Trade Paperback ISBN 978 1 444 74277 0
Ebook ISBN 978 1 444 74279 4

Typeset by Hewer Text UK Ltd, Edinburgh
Printed and bound by Clays Ltd, St Ives plc

Hodder & Stoughton policy is to use papers that are natural, renewable
and recyclable products and made from wood grown in sustainable
forests. The logging and manufacturing processes are expected to
conform to the environmental regulations of the country of origin.

Hodder & Stoughton Ltd
338 Euston Road
London NW1 3BH

www.hodder.co.uk

For Meredith, with all our love

Contents

'Remember you are never alone,
I am always with you, when you roam.
So close your eyes, I'm with you still.
I haven't left you, I never will.'

Stephanie Kercher, 'Don't Say Goodbye'

Foreword

On 1 November 2007, my daughter Meredith, who was twenty-one years old, was murdered in her bedroom in the cottage in which was living in Perugia, Italy, where she was studying at the town's University for Foreigners. In the days that followed, one of her housemates, an American girl named Amanda Knox, a young Italian man named Raffaele Sollecito and Rudy Guede, a Perugia resident originally from the Ivory Coast, were arrested on suspicion of her murder.

While Guede remains imprisoned for taking my daughter's life, in October 2011 Knox and Sollecito had their convictions quashed on appeal. My family and I now find ourselves in a limbo that, I suspect, might never end, wondering exactly what happened in those last moments of Meredith's life, and how convictions that seemed to offer all the terrible answers two years ago have now been so emphatically overturned. With Knox and Sollecito now free, we find that we are still waiting for justice for our daughter and sister, and have to face up to the stark possibility that we might never have a satisfactory picture of what unfolded in Perugia on that terrible November night.

I thought long and hard before putting pen to paper and beginning to write this book. At first, I wasn't certain if it was the right thing to do. Nor was I certain if I could do justice to her. It was a difficult decision, one I laboured over, and one that I could not have taken without the full support of Meredith's mother, her sister Stephanie and her brothers John and Lyle. Perhaps, I thought, the process of writing might be too painful. Everything was too close to the moment, the events still vivid, the memories too personal. It was not an easy task to confront. For a long time I had toyed with the idea of writing down everything that had happened as a personal memento for our family, something we could carry with us as the years progressed, so that we might never forget exactly what our daughter and sister was like. Then, many of Meredith's friends, her teachers, her school and university associates and the girls who had known her in Perugia told me that I had to put something down in book form – not just for my family, but for everybody else as well. Despite everything that has happened since that night in November 2007, it still seems as though nobody knows anything about the real Meredith, and my hope is that, through writing *Meredith*, I can share with the world something of the wonderful girl who was our daughter and sister. Tragedies can drive people further apart, but in our case, although Arline and I had split up long before Meredith was killed, we have all coped with this horrific ordeal as a family. Throughout, we've shared a determination to support each other, to honour Meredith and celebrate her life. Naturally, the last four years have been the worst of times for us, and I hope that telling the world about the enchanting, generous, kind person that Meredith really was can help those whose lives she touched. Though nothing can take away the pain of losing her, writing about her and talking to so many of her friends throughout the writing process has certainly been a great help to me. I also hope that this book might help to keep Meredith's case in the spotlight, and, in some small way, to keep alive the hope that we might yet know the truth about her death.

The media's glare throughout the trial and appeal process has been fixed almost entirely on the accused. It has seemed as if Meredith has been all but forgotten as the victim. In writing this book, then, I hope to go some way towards offering Meredith a tribute – for Meredith was a beautiful, intelligent and caring girl whom everyone loved, and her story deserves to be told. As her sister Stephanie said at her memorial service: 'Anyone who was fortunate enough to have known her would testify that she was one of the most caring people you could ever meet. Nothing was too much for her. She was a loyal daughter, sister and friend.'

Writing this book has been a journey not only of rediscovery – of long-forgotten memories of the Meredith we knew and loved – but also of discovery. Along the way I have met with many of Meredith's friends, and heard so many stories about her that still live on. I met with friends from her schooldays, many of whom I already knew and with whom Meredith stayed friends after she left home to study at the University of Leeds. I met with the new friends she made as a young woman in Leeds, where she studied for a degree in European Politics and Italian, most of whom I had not encountered before, and with whom she had shared a house. Many of her closest friends met me for a coffee in London, where they recounted their memories of her. Most of the stories were extremely amusing and often gave me an insight into Meredith that even I might never have known. I had no idea, for instance, that she was such a good dancer; though I had seen her at her ballet classes, I had never imagined her on a dance floor, dancing to her favourite 1980s music. By meeting Meredith's friends, from all the different corners of her life, I was able to paint a portrait of the girl we have lost.

I met with Meredith's teachers, too. When speaking to the Italian teacher from her old school, I was to learn just how much Meredith enjoyed the trips she had taken with the school to Italy. I was also to learn from her how deeply her teachers respected Meredith, and how they even thought of her as an 'intellectual'. I knew how bright and intelligent Meredith was, but hearing that word took things to a different level, and even changed my perception of her. It was only when Meredith's university teachers and her fellow students spoke of the things that Meredith had achieved with the

Italian language that I began to realise what her Italian teacher had meant.

Later on in my writing, I was to meet with the English girls who had met Meredith in Perugia. They had only known her for a couple of months, but they had already established that Meredith would be a friend for life. She had that effect on people. It was not simply that she was good company and fun to be around, it was how much she cared about people and how she was always prepared to devote time to them to help advise them on any problems they might have had. She was someone you could count on.

The girls who Meredith met in Perugia took the time to come from their homes around England to meet with our family on several occasions, and we really appreciated that. They still stay in touch, and we appreciate that, too.

Our family know how special Meredith was – but so many others, who never met or knew her, seem also to have captured in their minds precisely what she was like, simply from seeing photographs of her. So often we have heard the same loving comments about her smile, the smile that engaged so many people and drew them to her to be her friend.

This has not been an easy book to write, but, as a collection of memories and stories about Meredith, I hope it is a portrait of which she would have been proud. I also hope that, for perhaps the first time, the story of the trial that resulted from Meredith's murder can be told, plainly and simply, without being the subject of tabloid fascination.

Recently, while cleaning my home, I came across an old shoebox, inside which I found roll after roll of undeveloped photographic film, many years old. Over the course of the last months I have slowly been getting the photographs developed – and, once again, I have been watching Meredith, Stephanie, John and Lyle as they have grown from babies, to toddlers, to children, and then to young women and men. In each photograph she has that wonderful smile and, sometimes, that funny smile, which I called her *Wallace and Gromit* look. Here were pictures of Meredith as a child that I had forgotten, little images to prompt even more recollections, and make us cherish even more the time we had together.

It is not only our family and her friends who have lost her. So has the world.

I

Meredith's Murder

1 November, 2.15 p.m.

I am in my local bank in Croydon when Meredith telephones me, to see how I am, from Perugia. The bank is relatively empty and I'm at the counter drawing out a small amount of cash. It is 2.15 p.m., an unusual time for Meredith to ring as we usually speak to each other in the evenings. Most days, I ring her at around six o'clock, before she goes out or settles down to study, and me calling her saves on her phone bill. Usually we chat about what she is doing, but today she does not have to go to the University of Foreigners, where she is studying European Politics and Italian, as it is a public holiday in Perugia and she has the day to herself. The university is said to be the 'oldest and most prestigious institution in Italy involved in teaching and research activities' and is attended by students from all around the world. Meredith has been studying there for almost two months. We chat for two minutes, but the call is

7

costing her money and I tell her I'll call her later. So we don't have a chance to say much. I tell her that I'll call her when I get home, but she says that she is going out that evening to have dinner with some English friends, so instead we arrange to speak the very next day. It is lovely to hear her voice in the early afternoon, especially knowing that I won't be chatting to her until the following evening.

I didn't realise that it would be the last time that I would speak to her. She told me she loved me and my final words to her were 'Love you too.'

2 *November, 5 p.m.*

I am at home when Meredith's mother, Arline, calls me to say that she has seen on the news that a female British student has been found murdered in Perugia. I have been divorced from Arline for ten years, and she is living in Old Coulsdon in Surrey. Obviously, Arline's call startles me. I am worried, but I tell myself that there are many British students studying in Perugia, and I try to use that as a calming influence. I promise Arline that I will try to get some more information.

Immediately, I ring Meredith, but in response I can get only an automated message. This is not necessarily unusual because, at that time of day, she could still have been at the university or in the library, and would have switched off her phone. Even so, I am naturally concerned. For the next half an hour, I try her number at least a dozen times, but every time the phone goes through to the automated message.

Suddenly, after what feels like an age of trying, her mobile starts to ring. Believing that this has to mean Meredith has turned her phone back on, I feel some relief and, for the first time, I am confident that my daughter is fine.

Yet, the phone rings on and on, and still there is no answer.

The unease as to whether Meredith is safe or not begins to return to my mind, but I assume that she might have been in a different room. All the same, I keep trying for a further half-hour. I must try more than a couple of dozen times, ringing every few minutes, getting more and more nervous with each call. Yet, I tell myself, at least the phone is ringing.

Knowing that I have to get some information, I decide to call the foreign desk of the *Daily Mirror*. Having worked as a freelance journalist for most of the national newspapers and magazines for more than thirty years, mostly writing celebrity interviews and general features, I assume that they will know who I am, and it seems to be the logical thing to do. A man on the other end of the line tells me that they only have sketchy details of the incident in Italy, but if I call back in an hour they might have further information.

When I do, after an agonising hour-long wait, I am told by one of the foreign-desk editors, whom I do not person-ally know, that the Italian police have found the British girl's mobile phone, and that they have been in touch with people in London. Again, my hopes rise, because this must mean that, whoever this unfortunate girl is, her family and the British police must have been notified. This makes me feel a little more comfortable, because if it was our daughter, then at least we would have heard something from the British Foreign Office.

I call Arline to tell her this information and she seems somewhat relieved. Even so, I cannot let myself believe that everything is fine, for the details are still sketchy. For the next half-hour I sit by the phone, just waiting, trying not to feel so extremely apprehensive. Then the phone rings.

The call is from the *Daily Mirror*'s foreign desk, from a young girl to whom I had not previously spoken. Hesitantly, she tells me that they have a name for the girl. Though I ask for it, she is reluctant to tell me. She seems somewhat nervous herself, and I have to persuade her to release the name.

I shall never forget her words.

'The name going round Italy,' she says, 'is Meredith.'

In that instant, I drop the phone. I do not believe it. There has to be a mistake. Totally numb with shock, I cannot even cry.

After I had composed myself, I knew that I had to head for Meredith's mother's home in Coulsdon. As I did not own a car, I called a friend, who quickly drove over to pick me up. Then, we were bound for Surrey. Sitting in the passenger seat, I refused to let the facts sink in. I repeated it over and over to myself: 'Not beautiful Meredith . . . Not beautiful Meredith . . .'

On the way, I telephoned the Foreign Office, to see if they could confirm what I had been told. Though they said that they did not have the full details, they did tell me that there was a possibility that the name 'Meredith' could simply have been on the mobile phone that the Italian police had discovered, and that I should not necessarily jump to conclusions. As we drove on, I started wondering if I really was just jumping to conclusions, but somehow I couldn't convince myself.

I arrived at Arline's house within an hour. Our entire family – Stephanie, John and Lyle – were already there. There was no need for me to tell them what the rumour was among the journalists; by now Arline too had spoken to the Foreign Office. They had confirmed the worst. While I had still been driving over, she had taken that terrible call, and had already broken the news to our other children. The dead girl was Meredith.

In the living room, everyone was crying. Yet I could not shed a tear. I was just too numb.

At 9 p.m., Meredith's picture came up on the news. I stared at it, registering its familiarity but unable to react. I could not believe that this was my daughter. I remember thinking that this news report could have been the first we would have known of Meredith's death, but for what had gone before.

Meredith, the newscaster reported, had died on the night of 1 November 2007, only twenty-one years old.

We stayed together until after midnight, when I went back to my own flat. Stephanie and Lyle stayed with their mother. I can't say how I passed the night, except that I don't think I slept. When I returned the following morning, the street outside the house was lined with photographers and members of the press. It was strange and unnerving having to walk through them. Although I had been a freelance journalist for many decades and had often been to press events, nothing prepares you for being on the receiving end of their attention, not under such dreadful circumstances. Not one of the reporters gathered outside knocked on the front door, seemingly out of respect for our grief, but several of them did put notes through the letterbox, saying that if we did wish to talk, we should ring the telephone numbers they supplied. Though their respect was comforting, they were still there for a story, and the mere fact that they were there was quite intimidating.

That morning, too, we were visited by a local female police liaison officer, who explained various procedural details to us. We were told that there might have to be two autopsies conducted on Meredith, the first by the police to determine the time and causes of her death, and a following one that might be requested by alternative sources. Of course, an autopsy is vital to establish the circumstances of death and help an investigation, but hearing about it is a brutal reminder of the physical realities of that death. It is one of those pieces of information you hold at arm's length, not daring to think about what it means for your child.

Stephanie told us that some of Meredith's old school friends were going to lay floral tributes at the gates of the Old Palace of John Whitgift School in Croydon, a public school set in an Elizabethan building, where Meredith had studied for eight years. As a family, we went to meet them. Driven in a police car, we were pursued by members of the press. It was quite nerve-wracking, as anyone can imagine, and I was constantly looking out of the rear window. All the same, we lost the press en route because we had a head start on them and the local police were obviously more familiar with the various routes to the school.

At the school gates, in a narrow road in the old town of Croydon, we were expecting half a dozen people, and were stunned to find more than seventy, many of whom had travelled from their various universities around the country. Every one of them carried enormous bouquets of flowers and many were in tears. Some I knew, while others were friends of Stephanie's. It was an extremely touching moment for all of us as one by one they hugged us and expressed their condolences. Meredith had clearly meant so much to them, and they to her.

We entered the small school gardens. Flowers and messages were being laid on the lawn near the headmistress's office. A small prayer was read by the school's curate, the Reverend Colin Boswell, amid the shock that was being felt by everyone present. Our family were scattered among their friends. Young men were crying.

The next few days were numbing and filled with disbelief. I spent each evening at home, but visited the family during the daytime. We did not want to believe that this terrible event had happened. I was tempted to telephone Meredith, simply expecting to hear her answer the call, even though I knew that she would not.

Two days later, a senior officer from London's Scotland Yard visited us to explain what the procedure in Italy might be. It did not appear that there was much information yet. I had no idea whether the British police were liaising with the Italian police and authorities, but, even so, they seemed to be aware of international procedures.

The man from Scotland Yard explained carefully, and with compassion, that, whilst an autopsy on Meredith's body was automatic, it might be that the lawyers representing the accused might request a further autopsy. As a result of this, we could expect a possible delay in Meredith's body being flown back to the United Kingdom for burial. At this moment, we had no way of knowing that it was going to be six weeks before we could lay her to rest.

Nor had we any idea how much the tragic loss of Meredith, under such dreadful circumstances, had touched the world. At my flat, I sat down in front of my computer and turned on the screen. My fingers hovered over the keyboard and I typed Meredith's name into a search engine, not knowing what I would find.

Rather than tabloid stories about her tragic death and the furore that was beginning to emerge regarding Amanda Knox, I discovered a tribute page filled with dedications people had written to her, some by those who had not even known her in life. Many were from old school friends, not simply those from Old Palace, but also her junior school, Keston, in Old Coulsdon. They wrote personally to her, as though she was still alive, often signing off with words such as 'I hope the angels are looking after you.' Others recalled memories of things they had done together, as though she were on the end of a telephone line.

Just as remarkable were the messages of sympathy that came from people who had never known her. The letters came from Brazil, Australia, the Netherlands, the USA and South Africa. Some were addressed to our family, others personally to Meredith, and so often these strangers would remark on her smile and what a beautiful person she seemed. Even in death, she reached out to people.

Sitting there, reading those messages, seemed to bring Meredith back for a fleeting moment: my daughter, alive, vibrant, laughing – I could almost imagine that I was about to hear her voice from another part of the flat.

Nothing can prepare you for what it is like to have to travel to a foreign country to identify the body of your daughter. After hearing the terrible news of Meredith's death, we waited almost a week to be able to travel. We had no idea what we were going to face when we arrived out there, nor what to expect.

I flew with Arline and Stephanie to Florence, to meet with members of the British Consulate. John and Lyle were unable to attend because of work commitments, and because of the cost of our travel expenses. Throughout the whole process we were to receive no financial help from our own Foreign Office, and had to find a way of funding everything ourselves. This was financially crippling, but something we just had to do.

From Florence, we had a high-speed, two-hour drive to Perugia. Perugia is the capital city of the Umbrian region, built on a high hill, and once the scene of a prehistoric settlement. It was conquered by the Romans, destroyed and, after many more conflicts across the centuries, became a powerful independent city state and a Papal State. Today, it is a thriving artistic and cultural centre – and as we approached, it was difficult to believe that this beautiful corner of the world was where my daughter had died.

Meredith had come here as part of her studies at the University of Leeds, where she was studying for a degree in European Politics and Italian. Meredith had always loved Italy. We would take her for Italian holidays when she was very small, and later she visited the country on school trips. Who knows what was going through her mind when she and our family first visited Italy when she was one and a half years old, and we wheeled her in the double pushchair with Stephanie through the streets of Rimini. But when she was eight years old we returned there, and she was much more aware of the place, with its history dating back to 286 BC, as well as the country and its people. She was extremely amused at the way the Italian waiters always offered her and Stephanie the menu before the rest of us and treated them like young ladies rather than children. The waiters would often wink at us as they went about this sophisticated routine. It was here that Meredith had her first taste of real Italian pizza, amazed at how the cooks made them in wood-fired ovens and retrieved them with long poles. And she always knocked her drink over; apparently, something she continued to do into adulthood.

All of this must have made a big impression on her, because when she entered senior school at the age of fourteen, she elected to study Italian, and later went on to study the language at Leeds University. For her year abroad, she contemplated going to Rome, Milan and Perugia, but after talking with various people she thought that Perugia might be a better choice. Being smaller, the medieval town would provide a greater opportunity for her to interact with other students and people. So she made her decision and had spent the summer looking forward to it with mounting excitement.

It was only a little more than two months ago that Meredith had moved to Italy. She had flown to Rome in late August with a suitcase full of clothes – and then found that the only way she could get to Perugia by train was via Florence, where she could pick up a connection. She made it, but later said that the journey had been quite arduous. Still, it meant that by the time she reached Perugia, she had negotiated her way through two of the busiest train stations in Italy, and had the satisfaction of arriving as an independent traveller among the steep, wooded slopes of Umbria.

On the telephone, she had told me how beautiful the city was. Now we were approaching it for the first time, and she was never coming home.

On the outskirts of the town, beautiful and hilly, we could appreciate why Meredith loved Perugia. We rendezvoused with the Italian police at a roundabout, and they gave us an escort to the morgue. They did not speak English, but the consulate staff liaised with them about our safest route, and acted as our translators. As we climbed upwards, however, our talk petered out as we all felt the incongruity of the beautiful scenery and our purpose for being there. Our daughter had been murdered here, in this most beautiful landscape.

At the morgue, a small number of the press kept their distance, taking their photographs, but several expressed their sympathies. Some had tears in their eyes, which was a touching moment for us. Inside, there were a large number of officials, including the Chief of Police in Perugia, Arturo De Felice, and the head of the Homicide Squad, Monica Napoleone. Many of them were close to tears.

It was time to see my daughter.

I couldn't go in. I had been so numb on the journey here that the brutal reality of having to see what had been done to my beautiful daughter had not really hit home. In the back of my mind, I supposed I had known why we were there, but now, only metres away, I could not face going in. I stood there, motionless, trying to explain that I did not want to go in and see Meredith. A small man from the mortuary approached Arline and Stephanie and, leaving me behind, they went through the doors. They asked me if I wanted to join them, but I could go no further. For me, it would have put a full stop to my memory of Meredith. I had seen her only a couple of weeks before, when she had flown back to London to buy some winter clothes. We had met for a coffee in a small Italian restaurant in Croydon, a place where we often met or had the occasional lunch. We would talk about books and music; the Italian film she had been to see at the university to improve her language skills; the occasional dance she had been to with the new English friends she had made; and the wonderful pizzas she was eating in the evenings.

On this occasion, Meredith had been almost an hour late, and I had sat in the restaurant waiting for her. (This wasn't unusual: Meredith would often overestimate how much she could fit into an hour, and end up late.) When she arrived, she talked eagerly about Perugia and how she was making herself at home. She said that she was trying to buy a duvet for her bed, to make her room cosy, but nobody seemed to know where she could find one. I remember her being amused by this, and saying she was determined to track one down. That this should be the duvet beneath which her body would be found is something that will always haunt me. Over lunch, she had shown me some boots she had bought. She had been laughing, and was happy. It was the last time I had seen her, and I wanted that to be the memory that I held in my mind for ever.

Whilst Arline and Stephanie were seeing Meredith in the mortuary, I stood with the Chief of Police in the large foyer. He did not have to say anything to me; his expression of grief said it all.

When Meredith's mother emerged from having seen her, she said that Meredith looked beautiful and peaceful. Arline even smiled once, as though all of the happy moments in Meredith's life were passing through her mind. Her neck had been covered, which was a blessing. At this stage, we only knew that her throat had been cut, causing her death. We had no idea that, as would later be revealed, she had suffered more than forty wounds prior to being killed.

In the morgue, standing over her body, Arline had said, 'Your father's come all this way out here to see you, but doesn't feel he can.' Then she had smiled, for the last time, at our daughter. 'But,' she had whispered, 'you know what your father's like . . .'

From the morgue, we were driven to be interviewed by the lead prosecutor, Giuliano Mignini. Mignini was an avuncular person, about sixty years old, who smoked a pipe and had, as I was later to learn, daughters of his own. He was serious about obtaining information on Meredith, and wanted to know in particular what she had told us of her housemate Amanda Knox. At that stage, although there had been a lot in the press about Amanda Knox and Raffaele Sollecito and their statements to police, we still thought of them as witnesses.

We knew they were being questioned, but it seemed part of the general maelstrom of police activity. I knew only little of Amanda, but could remember that Meredith had said that the American girl was eccentric. I sat alone in a large room with only Mignini and a young man who was typing and recording our conversation, and struggled to answer his questions as best I could. After my interview, it was the turn of Stephanie and Arline.

Once we were finished, we went to our hotel for the first time, a large building with a balcony overlooking the surrounding countryside and the hills dotted with houses. For our first visit to the place where Meredith had died, the mayor of Perugia had kindly arranged a peaceful place for us to stay. Knowing, from what we had been told by the consulate, that we had to deliver a statement to a press conference later that evening, we were wary. This was an idea none of us had entertained before, and we did not know what to expect from it. We would have to talk about Meredith to people who didn't know her; how could we find the right words to do justice to her? It felt terribly important not to let her down, but we were all shattered and still in shock, and we didn't know what their attitude would be.

At the hotel, the press photographers were waiting. They snapped pictures of us arriving, walking through the foyer and even while we stood in the elevator, waiting for the doors to close. They were scrambling over each other to get their pictures, and Arline, Stephanie and I were all unnerved.

Later that evening, we were led downstairs into a small room adjacent to a conference room, where we were introduced to the mayor of Perugia, the head of the University for Foreigners, and the British ambassador to Rome. They were all middle-aged and reverential. All seemed in a state of shock and close to tears. The mayor, a small and kindly man, held my hands and looked into my eyes with pity. A press officer from the British Embassy translated their sympathies to us.

Emerging from the elevator for the press conference was like nothing we could have fully anticipated. A barrage of cameras, flashing like strobe lighting, exploded before us. The photographers ran alongside us until, eventually, I suggested that we simply stood still for a few minutes to try and control the mayhem. Arline and Stephanie seemed as bewildered by it all as I was.

Some ten minutes later, we were sitting at a long table in a conference room. Here, we were confronted by the world's press: American, British and Italian film crews and dozens of cameramen. We were not in confrontation with these people, who were only doing their jobs, but all the same we did not know how to react. Sixty or more cameramen, some only a foot away, thrust zoom lenses into our faces, while television cameras rolled in the background. It was a disquieting experience – yet, within all this mayhem, I could sense how much they felt for us.

Eventually, the room went quiet, and Stephanie bravely read the statement she had prepared for the press. She had written it only a short while before, and because she can speak Italian, she read two versions of it.

'Mez,' Stephanie began, 'as she was fondly known to us and her friends, was someone special, who worked hard and cared about people.

'As anyone who was fortunate enough to have known her would testify, she was one of the most beautiful, intelligent, witty and caring people you could ever meet. Nothing was too much for her. A loyal daughter, sister and friend.

'She was excited at the prospect of spending a year in Italy, making new friends and immersing herself in the culture. She was pursuing her dreams. We can take comfort from the fact that she passed away at what was one of the happiest periods of her life.

'It is no exaggeration to say that Mez touched the lives of everyone she met with her affection, personality, smile and sense of humour.

'The sheer volume of tributes that poured in during the days following her passing bear testimony to the special girl we'll always remember.

'We loved her then, we love her still and she is still very much a part of our family for ever.'

It was a beautiful and moving speech and I felt so proud of her. Although the journalists had never met Meredith, I felt that Stephanie's words brought a vivid impression of her into that crowded room.

When the press conference was completed, we were exhausted from the travelling and the meetings, and the strain of talking and listening through our grief. A quiet dinner had been arranged for us in a private room, a refuge from the frantic activity. We ate with two members of the British Consulate and the British ambassador and in honour of Meredith, who was so full of life, we tried to create a light-hearted atmosphere. It was a way of paying tribute to her. We talked about her and even raised our glasses to her. This is something we shall always do on every one of her birthdays, because Meredith's memory remains with us so strongly – and I hope that, somewhere, she knows this is so.

The following day, we visited the church in Perugia's main square, where so many of her friends from the town had lit candles for her, and left our own. I wondered if Meredith herself might have visited this church, and whether we were walking in her footsteps. Then, British Consulate staff drove us back to Florence, where we met and hired the services of a lawyer, Francesco Maresca. We had been presented with a list of lawyers by the consulate, and we felt that he seemed the most suitable. He was young, experienced and would be able to update us on what was happening when we returned to England. Without him, we would have been very much in the dark. This was essential, because we needed someone of that legal calibre to represent our interests and to keep us regularly informed as to what was happening. He was in a position to liaise with all the necessary people and authorities, and communicate to us on a regular basis.

From there, we took the flight home, preparing ourselves

for the long wait before Meredith would be returned to England and we could finally lay her to rest. We could barely breathe a word to one another during the flight, and even when we did get back to England we were too stunned for a few days to discuss anything. Though still shell-shocked, only after those days had passed were we finally able to talk to John and Lyle about our trip to Perugia, and begin discussing what might have happened on the night of Meredith's murder. At this stage not many details had emerged, and in any case, we couldn't bear to speculate much; for the most part we only wanted to talk about our memories of Meredith. But we never imagined that it would be six long weeks before she would be flown home.

2

Our Beautiful Girl

Being back in England, after the traumatic experiences of Perugia, was a difficult and confusing time. Everything seemed unreal. There wasn't a second that passed when I didn't wonder if this had all really happened, or question why. I would look at a photograph of Meredith, and believe that she was still here. Her face was everywhere – on the television, in the newspapers – and it was as if I was reading about someone else. Then, every time, there came the terrible realisation that this was real, that my family and I were trapped in a living nightmare. I kept trying to convince myself that she would one day be coming home.

Of course, we knew that when she returned, it would be for her to be buried in peace.

On the night that we came back to England, I went home to my flat and Stephanie stayed with her mother. It must have been tough for both of them, because they had seen Meredith at the mortuary, whereas I was still clinging to my memories of her alive. I could still see her smile and hear her laugh.

We spoke to John and Lyle about the trip to Perugia. At the time, John was working in electronics, setting up outside broadcasting systems, and Lyle was working in advertising. Their companies had both given them compassionate leave for a week, and it seemed as though they felt they had to be stoic about the events, being the other two males in the family. Although they spoke to their mother and tried to comfort her, comfort was a thing that none of us could get.

Stephanie and Meredith had always been incredibly close – and, indeed, Stephanie still feels close to Meredith, even after all this time. They loved and valued each other, and were friends as well as sisters. As Stephanie has said: 'Meredith never knew how effortlessly beautiful she was.'

And Meredith felt the same way about her sister. When Stephanie was working at a health club for a promotions agency at which she worked part-time, Meredith said to me: 'The girls are going to be drawn to her to sign up for the health club because they would want to be like her, and the men are going to be drawn to her stand because she is so attractive.'

I told Stephanie what Meredith had said, and she was really touched by it, but it was little consolation.

However, our attentions were now focused on the constant possibility that one of the defence teams representing the accused would demand a second autopsy on Meredith. This, they were arguing, was to try to determine the precise time of death. One autopsy was enough to contend with in our minds; a second was a prospect that we did not want to think about. To our relief, the request was denied. Yet it would still be six long weeks before Meredith would be returned to us to be laid to rest.

It was a dreadful period in our lives. Not one of us could comprehend why this had happened, who could have done such a terrible thing to such a beautiful young woman and for what reason. Graphic images kept invading my mind, even though, at this stage, we were not fully aware of the horrific facts of her death. All we knew was that Meredith had died from a knife wound to her throat. This was bad enough, but we were later to learn that she had actually sustained forty-seven other bruises and cuts prior to her death as she had fought for her life. I am glad we did not know at the time, for I do not know how I might have responded.

Stephanie was devastated by the events. She wrote, 'From the moment that we received the call about travelling to Italy, soon after her passing, I knew that we had to go and look after Mez. I can't even begin to imagine how my parents felt. I simply know how numb I was and how my mother's sudden strength pulled us together.

'I still remember looking at Meredith lying there, so still, no breath to be taken, a crisp white sheet pulled up to and over her neck. She seemed peaceful, yet she bore a look of determination, of courage marred with defeat. It was a look that let us know how hard she had fought to be with us, and for that, I am eternally grateful and love her more than she could ever know. It was from that moment that we knew we had to fight for her too. Not only for justice for her, but every day for ourselves for her.

'She really did touch so many lives with her selfless compassion and loyalty to others and continues to do so now. Nothing was ever too much trouble for her, and she would go out of her way to please everyone and look after everyone. Mez was my little sister, but she also cared about me and our family like an older sister. Meredith never knew how much of an impact she had on people. This was a quality of hers, which enabled her to make others laugh, help others when they needed someone to be there and become someone, without recognition, to aspire to. Meredith had such an incredible presence that the void she has left us with is noticeable every day.'

Meanwhile, the Internet tributes kept flooding in, and there seemed to be a rush of new posts when we returned from Perugia. So many uncannily captured her personality. Our local newspaper, the *Croydon Guardian*, had set up a tribute site, which I logged on to, and there must have been almost a hundred messages there. As the days went on, so the numbers grew and grew, and I quickly realised that this was on a global scale. People seemed devastated by this waste of such a beautiful young life. As they began to learn more about Meredith as a person, some were even saying that she was going to change their own lives, that they realised it was important not to be so self-centred, but to care and help others. It was extremely touching and comforting to read these things.

Yet still the torment of when she would be returned to us carried on. There were no definite dates, only delays.

Letters arrived at Meredith's mother's door from complete strangers, along with flowers, something which continues to this day. When Arline first called to tell me that these floral tributes were arriving, I made a trip to the house and saw that the living room was piled high with bunches and vases of flowers. It looked like a florist's shop and their perfume filled the air. There were also large bouquets and potted plants from national newspapers and television programmes, along with notes expressing their condolences. Arline kept a lot of the small message cards attached to the flowers, many from people we did not know. Knowing that friends and strangers were thinking of Meredith and our family brought us some comfort during a horribly bleak time.

At a Mexican-style restaurant, Conchitas, in Croydon, where Meredith had done part-time bar work during her return trips from Leeds University, the managers had placed a photograph of her together with a collection box on the bar. A couple of the chefs put their entire week's earnings into that box. They had been good friends with Meredith and had always insisted that, when she finished work, they should stand with her at the bus stop. Sometimes they would wait for more than half an hour, simply to ensure that she safely caught her bus.

It was moments like these that made me fully understand how Meredith had touched the world while she was still alive, and set my mind to wondering what impact she might have made if she had been allowed to carry on living. Naturally, thinking like this, my thoughts began to turn to her life and what a happy child she had been. I would find myself lost in memories of her jokes, her wicked one-liners and humour, her laughter, and I would immerse myself in old photographs of her early life. In one photograph I particularly loved, Meredith was opening her Christmas presents by the large fireplace in one of the living rooms in our old house in Coulsdon. It was funny how vivid the memories suddenly were. I remembered that, if we had a coal fire going, then on Christmas Eve I would pull some ash into the fireplace and draw small footprints with my finger to show that Father Christmas's boots had landed there as he climbed down the chimney. Meredith and Stephanie would put out a glass of sherry and a mince pie for him – but when they put out a carrot for the reindeer, that was a bit too much for me!

Meredith was almost a Christmas baby. In December 1985, we were all sitting at home in our house in Old Coulsdon wondering if she was going to arrive on the same day as Father Christmas. But, as was to be the pattern for her later life, she was late, and it was three days later, on the twenty-eighth, that Arline was taken to Guy's Hospital in London.

It was not until about six o'clock in the evening that I received a phone call to tell me that we could go to the hospital to be there for the birth. So I set out in the car with John, Lyle and Stephanie to drive the eighteen miles there. They were only nine, seven and two years old at the time, but, sitting in the back seat, they were all excited at the prospect of this new addition to our family. None of us had any idea whether they would be getting a sister or a brother; when Arline had her scan, we had told the doctors we did not want to know the sex of the baby, so that it would be a surprise.

The weather was freezing cold and, after about ten minutes, there was a loud rattling sound from under the car bonnet. Stopping at the side of the road, I discovered that the cooler water had frozen into chunks of ice. At first, I had little idea what we would do, but nothing was going to stop us from reaching the hospital on time. We abandoned the car and dashed to the nearest station, which was Purley, to continue our journey by train.

On board the rattling train, John, Lyle and Stephanie were nervous, and perhaps even a little confused. At this stage, not knowing the sex of our newborn, we had not chosen a name. For our first child, Arline had picked the name John, after me. Lyle's name had not been chosen until he was two weeks old, and was inspired by the scientist Lyall Watson, who had written the book *Supernature*. I myself had picked Stephanie's name, after the American actress Stefanie Powers, again with a different spelling. I think that Arline had wanted to call her Lucy – but, by the time she was born, I had convinced John and Lyle that her name was Stephanie, and it stuck. The name for our fourth child would have to wait until after she was born, and it was one that Arline and I settled on together, picking 'Meredith' from a book of baby names.

On our arrival at the hospital, we made our way up to the maternity unit, where a matron abruptly told us to go and wait downstairs. I explained to her that Meredith would probably be born within twenty minutes from the onset of labour, just as her sister had been. The matron looked at me as if I was ridiculous, and implied as much, insisting that we return an hour later. With the children in tow, I beat a retreat, found a canteen to get a sandwich and a drink, and then returned one hour later. When we did, the matron looked at me sheepishly and said that I had been right all along: Meredith really had taken only twenty minutes to be born. I would have loved to see her being born but, in the circumstances it was not possible.

Meredith was not a premature baby, but she only weighed 4 lb 12 oz. She was so small, I could practically hold her in one hand, and we had to buy special baby clothes and nappies for her called the 'Doll Range'. Later, when I saw her being bathed, I was amazed at how small she was. I remember picking her up and she was so slippery she almost fell out of my hands.

I like to think that it was because of the season she was born in that Meredith loved winter so much, especially when it snowed and she could get her plastic sledge out and whizz down the slope in the garden, or make a snowman. Nor did she mind occasionally walking the mile uphill to school with her mother, beside three-foot snow drifts, when it was impossible to drive her there. Or we would go to a large open area in Old Coulsdon called Happy Valley, a park with 1,500 acres of snow that Meredith loved to play in.

As she grew older, one bone of contention was that Meredith's birthday was only three days after Christmas. On everyone else's birthdays, we usually went to a restaurant for a meal, but no one in the family was capable of eating out after enjoying so much food at Christmas. So we did something in the New Year for her. It was the same with her birthday party. Because Stephanie's birthday was in the summer, she was always able to have her party in the garden in the sunshine. So we would arrange an event for Meredith in the warm weather, so that she could invite her friends around for games in the garden.

One thing that she did love, from about the age of three years, was bedtime stories, and I used to try to make them up for her and Stephanie every night. One was about Meredith going to a forest, where she would meet a fairy. The fairy would spin several times, then there would be a flash of light and Meredith would be transported with the fairy into an adventure.

Quite often the story would begin in the same way, and on one occasion I started the story as usual, and when the fairy had done her spinning I asked Meredith what happened next. 'She was sick because she was dizzy!' she replied and then laughed. Her unique humour surfaced at an early age.

Stephanie's own story was about being transported on a bird's back across forests and fields. There was never any jealousy or animosity between them. They would lie there, listening and giggling or adding bits to the stories. They really got on well together, and even as they grew older they would share confidences, along with clothes and cosmetics.

I must have stopped telling these stories when Meredith was about ten years old. One evening, when she was about fourteen, I was visiting her at the house she lived in with her mother and Stephanie. As I was about to leave, she asked me to tell her a story. I hadn't done this for some years, and said that I had told her so many I had run out of ideas. But she was quite insistent. Unable to resist, I said that when I got home to my flat, I would try to write something and read it over the phone to her. She was satisfied with this, and that's exactly what I did.

As usual, I made Meredith the central character, and wrote about 500 words. When I read it to her, she wanted me to continue with it and so, every day, that's what I did. Even when I went to Spain for a week, I would write some of it on the beach and then call her from a payphone in the evening and read it to her. Eventually, it became a 60,000-word novel, which I gave to her. It is called *The Strange Case of Miss Carla*.

The character of Miss Carla was based on an elderly lady, Muriel Babot, who lived on her own in the house next door to us when Meredith was young. She became like a grandmother to Stephanie and Meredith, as they did not have one of their own. They adored her, and she was always inviting them into her home, where she would make them do jigsaw puzzles with her. She would also come to our house to babysit occasionally, but she was weak, and I would have to help her through the garden to our front door. Yet the girls loved her looking after them, and she would often bring photographs for them to look at. She had a wonderful sense of humour.

In the novel, Miss Carla is quite a mystical character, and she travels through time, becoming younger as Meredith becomes older.

Mrs Babot's son-in-law, Paul, was a steam railway enthusiast, and lived only a few miles away. He had transformed his garden in such a way that miniature railway tracks ran all the way down and round it, with proper signals and lights. He had several trains powered by steam, and he would sit on the engine and people could sit on the back. Several times each year he would hold an open day and other enthusiasts would bring their engines, too, which would be put on the tracks. We were always invited, and Stephanie and Meredith loved riding around the garden.

In October 1987, when Meredith was nearly two years old, a hurricane came through Old Coulsdon. At the time, Meredith shared a bedroom with her sister in the rear of the house. What started as a fierce wind soon turned into a terrifying hurricane with 120 mph gusts, something most people in our country had never experienced. Realising the danger, we got the girls out of their bedroom, along with

John and Lyle, who were nine and seven, and we all huddled on the upstairs landing, with the bedroom doors shut. Huddled there together, the boys were quite protective of their sisters. Soon after we had hunkered down, there was a crash of glass as an eighty-foot tree slammed across the back of the house, a long branch breaking free and smashing through the girls' bedroom window. It was a fortunate escape. When the hurricane had subsided, Meredith, even at that young age, was stunned by the devastation outside, where another five giant trees had fallen and now crisscrossed the garden. In the road, trees were lying everywhere. I think that it was a sight she never forgot.

The following summer, there were still piles of bracken and tree branches in the garden, so we made a bivouac on the lawn that Meredith loved playing in. By the Halloween of 1988, she was asking me to make her a motorised witch's broomstick. It was the wish of a two-year-old girl. Of course, a motor was impossible, but I managed the basic broomstick, and I can still remember how happy she was while playing with it.

Sadly, Mrs Babot became extremely frail and had to go into a nursing home, where we visited her. Eventually, she passed away. Meredith often spoke of her, and the memories always brought a smile to her face. At her funeral, the priest, who spoke in a voice similar to the late American beat poet Alan Ginsberg, said that Mrs Babot had always enjoyed the company of Stephanie and Meredith, which really pleased them. Meredith and Stephanie had been such amusing and delightful company for her, and yet neither of them realised how much, even at their young ages, they had touched other people's lives.

In those days following Meredith's passing, looking at old photographs of her, other memories began to come tumbling back.

When Meredith was about five years old, her brother Lyle, then twelve, was a fan of the American band Guns N' Roses. The lead guitarist, Slash, was known for wearing a kind of stovepipe hat, as well as for shoulder-length hair that completely covered his face when he bent forward, and a cigarette hanging from his mouth.

I vividly remember one occasion when Meredith had just had her hair washed and it was long and fluffy. Picking up a toy guitar, she slung it around her neck, stuck an unlit cigarette into her mouth, put a hat on her head and then leant forward, so that her hair tumbled over her face. She was a double for Slash.

Meredith loved her ballet classes at the Parkinson School of Dance in Old Coulsdon. She started taking classes when she was six years old, and really looked forward to her classes every week. She was always excited when she had to do her grade exams and never seemed nervous. She and the other girls would all be in the dressing area in their pink ballet dresses and shoes, having their hair brushed back tightly and fixed with hairspray, and she was always pleased when she passed.

One weekend, the ballet school arranged for a dance troupe to come and teach the students one of the routines from the Andrew Lloyd Webber musical *Starlight Express*. With the professional teachers on roller skates, Meredith, Stephanie and the other girls were taught how to perform one of the show's numbers. The rehearsals took up most of the day, and then, in the late afternoon, we could all go and watch the finished article. Meredith loved it.

There was a similar event in our local theatre in Croydon some years later, when visiting actors taught youngsters how to do a song-and-dance routine from the musical *Grease*. Meredith really enjoyed that, too, because she was always a fan of musicals like *Flashdance* and *Strictly Ballroom*. Meredith never expressed a wish to become a performer, but at an amateur level she always liked to be involved.

Because of her love of musicals, Meredith, Stephanie and I often went to see stage shows. We went to see productions like *West Side Story*, *Cabaret* and *Chicago*. A highlight for her was when I got complimentary tickets from a press agency for us to go and see the legendary Liza Minnelli in concert at the Royal Albert Hall in London. We had a seat in a box and when Liza sang a medley from *Cabaret*, Meredith's jaw dropped. 'She is amazing,' she said to me. After the concert, because the press agency had arranged it for us, we went into a private backstage room where Liza was standing, chatting to other celebrity figures such as Joan Collins. Possibly, at that moment, Meredith really did harbour a wish to perform. I remember her eyes darting around the crowded room and seeing Liza's then husband, David Gest, poking his head round the door.

When Meredith was about fifteen we went to our local theatre in Croydon to see the American girl group Sister Sledge. I had met and interviewed them several times over the years and was quite friendly with them. So, after the show, we went backstage to meet them and then, later, joined them on their tour bus. The girls started to tell me where they would be each night, and Meredith said to me afterwards: 'You must be friends with them if they told you everywhere they are going to be.' I had to explain to her that everyone would know, as it was only their tour schedule!

Meredith always liked going to the coast, and as we were only a short drive from Brighton it was a place we visited regularly. Sometimes we had a picnic on the beach but at other times we would go to a restaurant that specialised in fish 'n' chips. Then there were the Lanes, a maze of narrow streets like a kasbah, filled with cafés, bistros and antiques shops. She was always fascinated by this place, and I often picture her there.

In 1997, Arline and I agreed to divorce, and I moved into a flat in Croydon. During that first week of living apart, I came home to find that Meredith had left a message on my answerphone, singing Whitney Houston's 'I Will Always Love You'. Her voice was beautiful and haunting, and I think that I cried on hearing it. It was so beautiful. I kept it there for as long as I could, playing it several times every day until the telephone service provider deleted it. If they had not, I would still be playing it to this day.

Meredith would come round to see me for dinner every Friday after school. It was always an exciting moment for me to look out of my window and see her in her school uniform, waiting to cross the road. I would cook dinner for us and then we would sit down to watch videos of the American comedy series *Friends*. She really liked the characters of Chandler, Joey and Phoebe. There was one episode that we particularly enjoyed and laughed at, where Joey is encouraged by the caretaker of his building to improve his dance techniques. It is hilarious to see Joey dancing with this other man, who wants to impress his dance partner, and to see how upset he gets when their dancing has to end.

I had over time bought six box sets of the show, which I was eventually going to give her because she could tirelessly watch episode after episode time and time again. Today, all those tapes sit on my shelf, a constant reminder of those happy evenings we spent together. With all of the regular repeats of the show on television, I am never far from those wonderful memories.

Meredith had an incredible memory, and I remember that once, when I missed one of the episodes of the show and asked her what had happened in it, she recited the whole half-hour of it, practically word for word.

One of the many things that Meredith loved was clothes and fashion. As a fifteen-year-old, like most girls of her age she looked forward to shopping. So, one day, I thought that she might like to go to the women's fashion department in Selfridges, on London's Oxford Street. I thought that she might like to spend about half an hour in there. How stupid of me! I should have taken a packed lunch. Despite the fact that there was nothing in her size, she managed to wander between the rails, picking up dresses, skirts, trousers and tops for a mind-boggling four hours, and I ended up sitting on a chair, exhausted, whilst I watched her merrily scrutinising everything. She loved every minute of it. This was her day. At last, we agreed on going for some lunch. When we had nearly finished eating, Meredith asked if we could, perhaps, go back into the store for a few minutes. One hour later, we re-emerged.

A more fruitful shopping spree was when Meredith, Stephanie and I travelled on Eurostar to the French town of Lille. Meredith was about fourteen and Stephanie sixteen. We had a wonderful lunch there in a small café, and then the girls discovered a couple of clothes shops that had everything in their sizes at incredibly cheap prices. I had to use the ATM machine across the road a couple of times to fund their purchases. From there, struggling with a number of classy-looking carrier bags with string handles, loaded with coats and skirts, we headed for the giant supermarket near the station, stopping at numerous shoe shops en route. The supermarket was my chance to grab some cheap wine and cheese, but we were getting close to the Eurostar departure time. We grabbed a supermarket trolley, piled everything into it and headed at speed for the station, laughing our heads off as we careered down a long, wide slope. Just in time, we managed to get on board the train and got everything home, where the girls spent the next hour trying on all their new clothes.

These memories kept piling on to me as we lurched from one day to the next, not knowing when Meredith was coming home, not knowing what had happened to her on that final night. Most memories reminded me of the good times, but there were some that brought me back to Meredith's final night, and all the unanswered questions we had about how she had died. I could not help thinking, for instance, of the hours Meredith had spent practising karate, and how she must have fought back on the night she was murdered.

I have to admit that when Meredith decided she was going to learn karate, it surprised me. She did not have any friends who were doing this activity. It was something she simply felt that she would like to do. She was about seventeen years old and it was the year before she accepted her place at Leeds University. The karate club that she joined in Coulsdon was up a long and winding country lane, near the stables where she and Stephanie had sometimes gone horse-riding when they were younger. Yet no matter what the weather was like, Meredith always made the effort to get to her classes. At the club, she trained against people of her own age, and also against men in their twenties and thirties, soon becoming capable of defending herself against someone twice her age. She once came to my flat and I asked her to demonstrate what she was doing in her classes. Her leg shot up and her foot brushed against my cheek. It was quite frightening, but demonstrated what she was capable of. I never saw her train, but Meredith was quickly on to her third belt in the sport, and she had set her heart on achieving a black belt at some time in the future. The future that she was never to have.

Now, facing up to her death, I could not help but think how those karate lessons might have served her on the night she was killed. There was no doubt, in my mind, that she could not have been overpowered by only one person – and I dared not imagine what her final moments had been like. When we later looked at the evidence that emerged from the police in Perugia, it was evident that there had to be multiple attackers in her killing. Against one person, we all were certain, Meredith could have held her own.

When Meredith eventually left home to study in Leeds, she joined a couple of promotions agencies, on a freelance basis, to help earn some money for her studies. Sometimes she was asked to promote various products, one of which was the Lynx brand. On one occasion she was working in Brighton for the product range when an Italian man approached her for directions. He was most impressed that she replied to him in almost fluent Italian.

Her major function with this agency was working at Gatwick Airport, where she worked on customer advice, directing passengers to their various flights. On one occasion there was a group of large rugby players who refused to respond to her polite requests to move away from a point of access so that passengers could move freely by. Undeterred, Meredith laid into them verbally, and onlookers were amused to see the musclebound sportsmen suddenly remember their manners.

The other promotions agency she had registered with had her photograph on their files, and so she was delighted when they rang her one day to ask if she would like to be considered for an upcoming music video.

She was excited about this, especially when she discovered that she was picked out of quite a few girls. The singer, in whose video she would appear in the lead role, was Kristian Leontiou. She knew of him, but had never met him. The song he was promoting was called 'Some Say'.

I took Meredith up to London for the filming at seven in the morning, when she joined a number of people and the film crew. It was a long day for her – it took almost fifteen hours to complete the video – and she was provided with a cab home. Later, she explained to me that it was nerve-wracking, not knowing anyone she had been working with.

In the opening shots of the video, Meredith is seen descending a staircase, and then later opening a swing door, through which she hauntingly walks.

Kristian Leontiou posted this message on his website: 'It has been brought to my attention by the UK media, that the young lady, Meredith Kercher, in my video, is the same young lady who was brutally murdered in Perugia.

'While I did not know Meredith, and only met her briefly, I would like to send my deepest and sincere condolences to her family and friends, while they go through this difficult and trying time. I can only hope that the video gives some solace, as it does seem to capture her true beauty, grace and charm.'

Watching the video now is an extremely moving experience. Our only other records of Meredith are our photographs, catching her in frozen moments of time. But in this video, we can still see her walking, moving, her eyes alive, as if she could reach out and touch us.

3

University

In 2005, Meredith was thrilled to be offered a place at Leeds University. She had worked hard to get the necessary qualifications, and was accepted for a degree course in European Politics and Italian.

Meredith had already visited the city, as her brother Lyle had gained his degree in media studies there. Also, she was aware of the excitement of university life, having been to see her other brother, John, at Warwick University, where he had studied electronics, graduating in 1997. Stephanie, too, was at university, studying in Portsmouth for a degree in marketing, which she would go on to achieve in 2006. All of this meant that Meredith was looking forward to both the studying and the social life. It would be a new experience for her, as none of her friends from school were going to the same university, but Meredith, as always, was looking forward to making new friends.

At this stage of her life, just eighteen years old, Meredith did not have a definite idea of what to do after she graduated. Once, over dinner at my flat, she hinted that she would like either to pursue a career in journalism, or to work at the European Parliament in Brussels. Whether journalism appealed to her because that was my career, I have often wondered, but she was certainly interested in what I did, and she had always loved writing. There was also a hint that she might, one day, love to live and work in Italy, but this would all be four years in the future, and for the moment they were just dreams.

Italy had always been important to Meredith. Her Italian teacher from senior school, Lucia Mazzeo, remembers how much Meredith enoyed learning Italian, right from the start of her lessons in Year Nine. She was already good at French – in fact Mrs Mazzeo had noticed that both Stephanie and Meredith seemed to have a natural flair for languages – but Meredith had quickly shown a delight in Italian culture and language. A year after beginning Italian, at the age of fourteen, the school organised a two-week exchange visit with Taddeo da Sessa school in the town of Sessa Aurunca, in the southern Italian region of Campania. Built on the southwest slope of an extinct volcano, fifty minutes from Naples, it is a beautiful, quintessentially Italian town, and has the ruins of a bridge with twenty-one arches and a Romanesque cathedral. The girls were to stay with Italian families whose daughters attended the Taddeo da Sessa school.

Mrs Mazzeo noticed how quickly Meredith fitted in, getting on well with Italian staff and students alike. 'They clearly fell in love with her smile, good nature and sparkling personality,' she told me. 'Her sense of humour was a factor too.'

As part of this trip, and a subsequent one three years later, Meredith and her school travelled along the beautiful and picturesque Amalfi Coast. They also travelled to Monte Cassino and to Rome, where Meredith's time management skills were put seriously to the test, fitting in visits to the Vatican, the Colosseum, the Forum and the famous Fontana di Trevi. Here, Meredith pledged her return to Rome by tossing a coin into the fountain, which, according to legend guarantees you will come back some day.

The party of English and Italian students, with extra friends, staff and even some parents, also visited Pompeii on their final full day in Italy. Pompeii was destroyed by the eruption of Mount Vesuvius in AD 79, and buried under volcanic ash for almost 2,000 years before it was rediscovered in the eighteenth century. It is a powerful place for anyone to visit, and it had a special meaning for Meredith because she knew Arline had done restoration work there in her youth.

The spectacular Caserta Palace, with its wonderful symmetrical gardens and 1,200 rooms, built for the Bourbon kings in the eighteenth century, also impressed her. Italy was everything that Meredith had expected it to be.

These exchanges were more than just sightseeing holidays: they gave the girls a real experience of Italian life. For two days on each visit, they became pupils at the Taddeo da Sessa School, where they were expected to attend lessons with their Italian partners, and even participate in sporting activities and drama presentations. Many of the girls bonded with their host families and for Meredith it was a transformative experience.

Mrs Mazzeo tells a story that I find very poignant. 'What I shall never forget,' she goes on, 'was the departure day from Italy, on Meredith's first trip to Sessa when she was fourteen years old. Almost all of the girls on the coach were crying. This was a difficult moment every year on these trips, as after being a part of someone's family for so long, saying goodbye was not easy. Yet we all noticed that Meredith was smiling. She didn't seem to be sad at all. I told her that she had the right attitude. Her reply was remarkable: "After this experience," she said, "I know that Italy is going to be a part of my life for ever. I'm not sad because I'm coming back this summer and, some day, when I'm older, I know that I am going to live here."'

Meredith was so taken with Italy that she asked us if she and a school friend could go back to the Italian family she had stayed with, independently, during the following summer vacation. We were a little apprehensive about the idea, as this would be the first time that she would travel abroad without the family or school, but by the time of her trip she would be fifteen years old, and she was already at that time quite a self-assured young woman. So Arline and I agreed, and flights were booked.

When the day arrived, we took her to the airport, where we met with her school friend, and you could see that she was excited. However, when we approached the check-in desk of the airline and the young woman looked at their passports, we were told that, being only fifteen, Meredith and her friend were too young to travel on their own, according to the airline's rules. The girls were devastated, but we discussed the matter later that day with the booking agent and found a new airline that would allow them to fly out the next day. Having made up her mind to go back to Italy, Meredith was not about to give up so easily.

Meredith's love of Italian was particularly illustrated by an incident that Mrs Mazzeo remembers with affection, and some awe.

'When she was in Year Thirteen, the modern languages and music departments at the school collaborated in a cross-curricular activity called "Light and Dark". This was intended to celebrate the music and poetry of the respective languages studied at the school. The Italian department contributed with three readings from Dante's *Divine Comedy*. Meredith was due to read one extract only, in Italian, from *Paradiso*. But a younger girl, who was due to deliver the *Purgatorio* reading, had a panic attack a few minutes before she was due to read, and so was unable to participate. In a very calm way, Meredith took over this reading and read it perfectly, without any practice at all.'

I love this story because it speaks to me so strongly of Meredith, but it has an extra significance for Mrs

Mazzeo, because of a strange incident that was to occur much later.

'The programme and scripts for this poetry and prose evening were mislaid,' she told me. 'I was not able to find them for years. Yet, a few weeks after Meredith's death, five years later, I stumbled upon the programme with her reading of Dante's *Paradiso*. Reading this extract has brought me some comfort during the most difficult moments following this terrible tragedy.'

As Meredith's teacher throughout secondary school, Mrs Mazzeo was able to watch my daughter grow from a child, through adolescence, into the beginnings of her life as a young woman with a bright future. 'In all of the time that I knew Meredith, I never heard her say one bad thing about anyone or anything. She never judged others and always tried to see the good side of people, even when we all nagged her about her timekeeping, and being late with assignments.

'Meredith was a popular, happy, good-natured girl, and I feel privileged to have watched her grow from a bright, enthusiastic eleven-year-old into a confident and intelligent young woman. I shall never forget Meredith. She will always be in my thoughts, and her memory will always be a part of my life.'

For Meredith, going to Leeds University was to be a new chapter in her life. She had spent the summer buying clothes and other things that she would need for her studies.

It was a sad moment for Arline, with whom Meredith had been living, when the day arrived for Meredith to leave. Yet it was also a happy one, for Meredith would be realising her dreams. We all wished her well. Though I was sad that I would not be seeing her every week as I had been used to doing, I was also excited for her.

Meredith loved Leeds from the moment that she arrived there. Leeds University, which was established in 1904, has ninety-three acres of campus, 33,000 students and libraries with more than three million books. The Department of Italian, which she attended, had 200 undergraduate students, and one of Meredith's lecturers was to tell us later: 'I have never known anyone make so many friends in such a short space of time. It was quite remarkable how her personality affected such a large number of students.'

For her first year, Meredith stayed in university accommodation on campus. 'It's a good thing to do,' she told us, 'as you get to meet a variety of people.' In her second year, as with most students, she moved out into private accommodation, having found a group of friends she loved to live with.

Two of these, Rosie Jones and Flick, have talked to me about their friendship with Meredith and their anecdotes give glimpses of the independent woman Meredith was becoming. 'I wasn't staying in Devonshire Halls where she was,' Rosie told me, 'but we had a mutual friend in Flick, whose flat was across the corridor from hers, and she was always popping over, and so we became friends.

I remember how she was really excited about showing us photographs of her then ten-month-old nephew, Max.' Max was Meredith's older brother John's son, and she adored him.

Flick remembers: 'It was whilst house-hunting after Christmas of our first year, and in subsequent run-ins with estate agents, that I was pleased to have Mez on my side. It took us a while trying to find somewhere suitable for six of us. That was Mez, Sarah, Maya, Flick, Susannah and myself. But eventually we settled on a property at 9 Brudenell Grove. Nobody really wanted the basement flat, but Meredith elected to be the inhabitant. She never complained.

'However, it was opposite the kitchen, and because she had taken an evening job in Vodka Revolution, a bar in town, she would often be coming in during the early hours of the morning. Sometimes, she would even be so late finishing work that she would already have been for breakfast with some of her work colleagues at a café. So, whilst we were having ours in the kitchen, she would appear bleary-eyed, nod to us, make herself a coffee and stumble off back to bed. She really worked hard to earn extra money for her studies. She would still be up and ready for her university lectures, although often late. But she did like cooking, and we shared our food.'

Hearing this made me smile because it brought back my own memories. Meredith would often ring me at home to ask for details of a particular recipe, perhaps from a meal we had enjoyed together at my flat, and then call to tell me if her friends at the house had enjoyed it.

'It is some of the memories of the everyday things that we did that I cherish the most,' Flick recounts. 'For instance, seeing Mez curled up on the sofa in the living room with all of her books around her, cooking big meals and watching lots of television.'

Rosie comments: 'There were a couple of soaps that we always tried to watch, dashing to the kitchen in between them to do our dinner.'

'Often big meals,' adds Flick.

'But then we did all go to the gym, once or twice a week, to keep fit and burn the calories off,' says Rosie. 'Nothing too strenuous for us. Usually, for Meredith and the rest of us, the running machine was the most popular piece of equipment.'

Whilst all of the girls liked music, and Meredith had always had a liking for 80s sounds, they did not go clubbing that much, because they had too much university work to do. Yet, as Rosie remembers: 'We would occasionally go to a nightclub at the University Union, which was called "Fruity", although it was a bit cheesy and uncool.'

They spent a lot of their time in the house chatting. 'I can't neglect to mention the hours that we used to spend playing Bananagrams,' Flick says, 'a crossword-type game, much to the bemusement of anyone who came round to see us.

'But Mez was an absolutely amazing friend. I don't think that you could put into words how much laughter we shared with her. Even mundane things like going to the shop down the road were made into incredible enter-tainment when we were all together.

'At the risk of making Mez sound like a bit of a geek, which I'm guessing everyone knows was definitely not the case, I have to say how much I valued her opinion on things. Whenever we chatted about something that was in the newspapers or on the news, she would always have something well-measured, unbiased and interesting to say.

'I guess that I appreciated her opinions because we agreed on a lot of things, which was pretty fortunate for me, because when you didn't agree with Mez, you were in for a persuasive argument.

'An amazing trait of hers was that she was supportive and willing to accompany you to things which you were interested in. For instance, I was always on the search for someone to watch the rugby on television with me, and Mez would always bring her duvet up to the living room to keep me company; even if she did fall asleep about twenty minutes into the game. During the rugby World Cup, she sent me a message saying that she had been watching England play and was falling in love with the game, which couldn't have made me happier. She said that she was very proud of our team and, in particular, Jonny Wilkinson.'

Another housemate, Sarah Carr, says: 'Whenever I think of Mez, I always picture her laughing. In fact, when I think of the year that the six of us spent together, nearly everything that we did resulted in laughter. Generally something ridiculous and immature, like a comedy sausage in a local shop, or a dubiously shaped vegetable that she would waggle in your face and snigger at. She had such a cheeky laugh, and it was completely infectious. When you were with her, you knew that you were going to have a fun night.

'Whether it was watching a film, or a night out dancing with friends, she could brighten up any event, and it would always undoubtedly result in us all being in fits of giggles over something so minor that other people would look on in confusion.

'I remember us ruining a tense watching of the film *The Omen* in our first year, by ripping apart the dialogue and the fashions. I'm certain that it annoyed everyone around us, but once we started, we couldn't stop.

'Obviously, some of our time was taken up with studies, although probably not as much as should have been. A major hobby of ours was going shopping as soon as our student loans arrived in the bank. And spending far too much money on fashions, then returning home to try on our clothes and justify the purchases to ourselves.

'Mez often worked evenings at a local bar, to get money for her studies, but on the nights that she wasn't, we would go into the centre of Leeds to see music or comedy, even the occasional play; but mostly to dance. We would spend ages at the house debating what to wear, and which of our many purchases would be best for the evening.

'She was always the last to be ready, and we would wait in the hallway, holding off taxis, to see her running up the stairs from her basement room, looking stunning, tottering around in her ridiculously high heels that she loved so much, but which really didn't mix well with cobbles or a Leeds winter.

'On nights in, we would watch television and gossip, whilst eating huge amounts of chocolate, or listen to music and dance around the living room. We were simply normal girls, enjoying the fact that we had a large house to ourselves. We would plan dinners together, traipse down to the local shops, and then cook up a feast. We developed quite a habit for drinking mulled wine in the winter, and I remember us brewing up a big jug of it before going for Christmas carols or to the Christmas market.

'We always tried to make the effort to spend time with each other, and went for a house meal at the end of each term – any excuse for a night out. Occasionally, we would have parties at the house too. In particular, we hosted the second anniversary of Glandfest, a tradition brought about in the first year at university, hosting a party for the day Meredith was allowed to drink again, after six weeks of abstinence, due to her suffering from glandular fever.

'We had been discussing it for ages, and Meredith was really excited about having everyone round. Unfortunately, it fell on a date when most of us had deadlines for university assignments, but we were determined not to give up. We arrived home from university at around 5 p.m., and began planning the event, running round the corner to find anything green that we could, as this was the theme for the party. We couldn't find any green food or drink, so we had to concoct a rather vile-looking red vodka jelly with tinned fruit floating in it. Throwing on our green clothes, we felt that we had failed Glandfest.

'But fortunately our guests were much more prepared, and soon arrived dressed in green, with face paints in hand and green drinks in tow.

'As well as being fun to be with, Mez was a really good friend and an intelligent and passionate person. She was also caring and considerate, never complaining about anything that upset her. She was tough, but would never expect the same strength from you. If life ever got too much, she would always be ready to let you crumple on her about the most trivial things. She was the kind of person you admired and were proud to have as a friend, always including you in the joke, and would make everyone completely at ease.

'Even though I only knew her for a couple of years, I feel like I have known her for ever, and throughout everyone's ups and downs at university, all the good memories that I have of the most intelligent conversations, the dirtiest jokes, the best nights out and, most importantly, the laughter and fun, they always include Mez.'

Before going to study in Italy, Meredith continued trying to earn as much as she could from part-time work. Her evening job was at a bar called Vodka Revolution, where she served drinks and was a delight to the customers. The manager often treated all the staff to a meal if the evening had gone well. Meredith frequently left her work at three or four in the morning, going with some of her colleagues for breakfast before heading home and getting ready for her morning university lectures.

Daniel Williams, who was working at Vodka Revolution, says: 'I remember that her sense of humour always made her stand out. I am certain that I had only known her for a couple of days when she brought me down a peg or two with a typically sarcastic and abrupt response to my attempt at trying to impress those around me.

'I was an old-timer at work too, and she was the new girl, so I thought that she had a lot of nerve. She always made us laugh, whatever ridiculous hour in the morning it was, and her smile is going to live in my memory for ever. I think that I speak for everyone who ever had the pleasure of meeting her, when I say that she'll truly never be forgotten.'

As well as working in Leeds, Meredith would look for work during her holidays to finance the term ahead. Indeed, it was on the recommendation of a friend that Meredith managed to get work as a tour guide, in the summer of 2007, on one of the open-top buses that show tourists around the major sights of London.

Jayne Moore, Central Operations Manager for the Original London Sightseeing Tour, has fond memories of Meredith. 'I interviewed her on 21 May 2007 for a seasonal job, as an open-top-bus tour guide in London. She had contacted the company via email, having heard about guiding from a friend of hers, Kayleigh, who had also worked as a seasonal guide. The job required candidates to participate in an intensive two-week training course learning about London history and its sights, followed by a three-month contract, after which she was going to resume her studies. I remember deciding fairly early in the interview that I would probably be offering her the job, because her manner was charming and unaffected, and I could see that she had the right personality for it.

'During the ten weeks that she worked for the company, she never complained, she was never off sick, loved getting a suntan and did a fantastic job. She was very enthusiastic and saw it as a great opportunity to learn about the history of London and do an exciting job during the summer break.

'Meredith started her contract in mid-July. I remember receiving a long text message from her on her first day of work that was obviously written in a state of distress, because she had been sent home for being late. Obviously, she might have thought that she would lose her job. It was raining that day, and I read the message on a phone that had raindrops trickling down it, as if she had been crying as she typed the message. She was never late again, and did a fantastic job telling tourists about London. One of the managers said that, quite often, when her tour had finished and the bus had pulled up to let passengers off, she would get a round of applause from them.

'She was popular with the drivers and other tour guides and, in early August, began to talk about an opportunity that had come up for her to go to Italy, as part of her studies. I was disappointed to lose a good tour guide, but pleased that she would be doing something so interesting. We discussed her coming back to work the next summer, and she said that she would be pleased to do so. I asked her to confirm her last working day in writing, and she sent me an email on 9 August saying: "*Hello, Jayne I would like it to be Sunday 26 August. Many thanks, Meredith.*" She returned all of her uniform to our head office a few days later, and talked excitedly about going to study in Italy.

'She was charming, because she was so unaffected and natural, and seemed to be happy all the time. She reminds me of the last few lines of a poem by Philip Larkin, which I copied out for my much younger sister when she was born. The poem is called "Born Yesterday", and the last lines describe:

> . . . *a skilled,*
> *Vigilant, flexible,*
> *Unemphasised, enthralled*
> *Catching of happiness . . .*

And I think that is what Meredith showed to the people who knew her and worked with her.'

I have often imagined Meredith on the bus, standing on the top deck, her face in the sun, or making a joke of it when the sky was grey or raining, and the passengers had to shelter under umbrellas. Meredith's friend Flick remembers the day that she, and a few friends from Leeds University, joined her on the bus for a tour.

'It was the last day I spent with Mez,' she says, 'and it was one of the best days I had. After lunch with friends in central London, Sarah, Rosie and I went for a ride on the tour. Although it was usually us berating Mez for being late, this time it was us who missed the bus and spent the next half an hour running around London, trying to catch up. When we did, she gave the most fantastic, witty tour, and even tried to force Sarah to give the bus a rendition of "Oranges and Lemons" when we passed the bells of St Clement's. The best bit had to be when she told an overeager American tourist to get back in his seat, instead of risking his life trying to get a photo of the London Eye.

'Unfortunately, it was at about this time that we got shown off the bus by the conductor, because of the not totally full-priced tickets which Mez had managed to get us. Later, we all met up for drinks and dinner, where we chatted about the coming year. Mez was so excited about going to Italy, and we all knew that she would thrive there, although we were going to miss her so much. I'll never forget the big hug that we gave each other, when we said goodbye . . .'

There were two ironic moments that prefaced Meredith's departure to Italy.

In the winter of 2006, Lloyd Thomas, then a nineteen-year-old dance teacher specialising in break-dancing, went to a Leeds University dance. 'I was doing one of my routines on the floor, and people were gathered around, as they do, when I looked up and saw Meredith, with some of her friends, starting to dance.

'I had seen her once, about a month before, and thought that she looked like a movie star, but I had not spoken to her. This time, though, I started talking to her. She was chatty and amusing, and at the end of our conversation, we exchanged telephone numbers. I called her later, and we decided to meet one evening on the steps of the university, which we did. We simply talked to each other for a long time.

'I went home, not knowing if our first "date" had gone well, but we got on fine. However, she did agree to meet me again. Surprisingly, we didn't kiss at all on those first couple of occasions. She was the first proper girlfriend I had had, and I don't think that I wanted to mess things up. Also, I was so taken with her amusing conversation, it might not even have occurred to me. But after our third date, we saw each other about four evenings every week and we were always together, although she had a lot of university work to do.'

Meredith went with Lloyd and his parents to a hotel called Ponden House, set in Charlotte Brontë country in West Yorkshire, for a weekend, and she really loved it. She rang to tell me how beautiful the scenery was.

'Meredith and I went there again, and I think that she found the half-hour walk from the bus stop a bit tiring,' remembers Lloyd. 'She never really spoke much about what she wanted to do when she graduated, but she had her heart set on going to Italy as part of her studies . . .'

After seven months of being with Meredith, certain thoughts were going through Lloyd's mind. 'I wanted to marry her,' he says. 'So, a couple of months later, shortly before her twenty-first birthday, I booked a table at a Japanese restaurant in Leeds, and proposed to her with a ring that I had bought. I think that she was somewhat surprised and didn't say yes or no. She kept the ring for a couple of days, but didn't wear it, and then she politely returned it to me.'

Inevitably, after she declined the marriage proposal, things were slightly different between Meredith and Lloyd. Meredith knew that it was not practical to get married so young, despite her obvious affection for Lloyd. She still had her current year at university to complete, a year in Italy studying, and then a further year of her degree, before she graduated. She was simply being sensible. Yet the two of them remained friends and a couple of weeks later, in January 2007, Lloyd joined our family and Meredith in an Italian restaurant in Croydon to celebrate her twenty-first birthday. Stephanie had arranged a special cake, with a photograph of Meredith as a one-year-old superimposed on it.

Who would have dared to think that this would be Meredith's last birthday?

There is another ironic touch to Meredith's strong desire to go and study in Italy. Originally, she had applied for a four-year course at Leeds comprising two years' study in Leeds, one year in Italy, then a further year back in Leeds. However, in the spring of 2007 she discovered that she had mistakenly been put on a three-year course that excluded the year in Italy. She was distraught at this, telephoning me and her mother almost daily to tell us about the problems she was encountering as she attempted to persuade her departments to rectify the situation.

One of the heads of department asked to see her recent Italian assignment and, seeing that she had only been awarded a C grade, told her that this was not high enough for her to be considered for Italy. Meredith explained that the reason for this was that she had handed her assignment in three days late. The tutor was surprised and knew that, according to university regulations, ten per cent of her marks had been docked for each day the essay was late. In fact, Meredith's work was of the highest quality and had earned an A grade. Eventually, after much discussion, it was agreed that she could go and study in Italy, and Meredith was overjoyed.

She was now faced with the choice of which city or town she should go to. She contemplated Rome, Milan and Perugia. After talking with various people, she decided that Perugia, being smaller, might be a better choice, and provide her with a greater chance to interact with people and students. For that simple reason, she decided on Perugia.

Meredith was excited when she was accepted by the University for Foreigners in Perugia, but confused as to where she was going to live for her year there. She spent weeks scouring the Internet trying to find student accommodation, but with no luck. She also had difficulty finding information about the course, only discovering after many calls and emails that she could go to whichever lectures she wanted, so long as she built up a certain number of credits. In the end, she decided that her best course of action would be to book into a small family-run hotel in Perugia for a few days and devote her time to finding suitable student accommodation.

She flew out to Rome in late August 2007 with a suitcase full of clothes and all of us wishing her luck. On the telephone that evening, she told me that it was lonely in her small hotel room and that she was probably going to go out and buy a pizza. Then, the next day, she was enthusing to us how beautiful the city was. It hadn't taken her long to settle in.

As ever, Meredith would call me every evening and we would talk about how she was getting on. I remember that she was particularly enthusiastic about the nine-day Eurochocolate Festival, due to be held in October in the centre of the city. Apparently it would stretch from Rocca Paolina to the Carducci Gardens, Piazza della Repubblica and Piazza IV Novembre. Later, after she had visited it, she told me that the festival had been wonderful, with dozens of different chocolate stalls and incredible chocolate sculptures that, towards the end of the festival, were broken up and pieces given to the public. She said that she bought me some of my favourites, which she would give to me when she returned home in November for her mother's birthday.

During her first three days, staying at the small hotel, she went daily to the University of Foreigners, or Università Italiana per Stranieri, searching the notice-boards for accommodation until, eventually, she found something promising. It was a white cottage with two Italian female tenants, somewhat older than her, and where an American girl was due to arrive a month later.

Meredith said that the Italian girls, Filomena and Laura, were friendly, and they took her to the landlord to help arrange things. Being in a foreign country, she felt a little uncertain and called me several times to check whether the amount of the room deposit was normal. After I had researched it, I called her back to say that it seemed like the usual procedure.

Meredith moved in to the cottage on the fourth day of her stay in Perugia, and set about making herself at home. We would talk almost every evening, as she did to her mother and sister. She would chat about books, music, Italian films and the English girls she had met, with whom she sometimes went dancing.

One of those friends, Natalie Hayward, recalls the first time she met Meredith. She had been studying history and Italian at the University of Sussex and says: 'I had chosen to study in Perugia because I had heard that it was beautiful and romantically old, in addition to being quite international. When I arrived, I managed to find accom-modation in an apartment with a couple of Italian girls.

When I began studying at the University for Foreigners, that was when I met Meredith and Amy Frost, the friend she had made. Because the three of us were the only English students in the class, we became known as "Little Britain".

'I didn't think that Meredith was English at first, as she looked Spanish or French; she had a Mediterranean look. But when I spoke to her and Amy and found that they were both English and staying in Perugia, I was pleased, because a lot of the students I had come to know were leaving. So it was really nice to have some new friends.

'I was so encouraged by the fact that Meredith accepted me, because I wasn't a particularly confident person. But she was always texting me to come out with her and other people and trying to include me in things, which I appreciated.

'It was always amusing how she would be late for lectures, but she was exceptionally good at taking lecture notes. You might not have thought it, but she worked so hard. I was jokingly jealous of her note-taking. The Italian lecturers would speak so quickly and be quite complicated, but Meredith could keep up with them. It was quite different from what we had come to expect at our respective British universities.

'Socially, Meredith was wonderful to be with. She was always smiling and making us laugh. She was never judgemental. And she and Amy would walk miles for a low-price meal! There was one student diner that was down a long hill, and they would travel all the way down and climb back up again for a meal that only cost a few euros.'

Following the tragedy of Meredith's death, Natalie returned to England to continue her studies and obtain her degree.

Helen Power was another British student who briefly became friends with Meredith, and she has fond memories of her.

'I first met Meredith on the night of 1 September 2007,' she says. 'I had just finished the August language course at the Università per Stranieri, and I had a day to relax in Perugia before flying home for a couple of weeks. In the hotel earlier that day I had met Amy Frost, a student from Leeds University, who was about to start the September language course. She invited me out for dinner with another student from Leeds, who she had yet to meet. So, that evening, we met by the fountain in the centre of Perugia, and it wasn't long before Meredith appeared through the crowd.

'As it was too early for us to eat, we sat outside and enjoyed some *aperitivi* from the cake shop on the main street. I remember that Meredith said she had forgotten to pack socks and that she hoped her dad would bring some out when he came to visit. Despite being tired from travelling, she was chatty, friendly, always smiling and making witty jokes. You only had to meet Meredith once to be struck by her beauty, quick wit and infectious smile.

'As the evening went on, our appetites got the better of us and we ate a huge dinner at Il Bacio restaurant. We had great fun getting to know each other, talking about home, university and life in Perugia. Meredith told us about how, in the summer, she worked as a tour guide on a bus in London, which sounded like an amazing experience. She had been learning Italian since she was at school, which was a great relief to me, as I had started learning it at university, and it was still rather rusty.'

Later that month, Helen's parents were with her for a few days and her mother, Sandra, says: 'Helen introduced Meredith and Amy to me at Piazza Italia in Perugia, as we waited to board the minibus on Friday 28 September. Meredith made a lasting impression on me as we chatted. Not only did she show a genuine interest talking to us, but she was so bubbly and full of life, with an infectious smile. I was so pleased to think that Helen had met such a delightful girl to be friends with during her Erasmus [the European student exchange programme] year.'

Helen says: 'The next time that we all met was at the Erasmus welcome meeting on 24 September. Our group of English girls expanded as we met people there. I was surprised that Meredith had noticed that I had had my hair cut. I thought that it was extremely observant of her, as she had only met me once, three weeks earlier. But that was the kind of girl she was; always making time for other people and taking note of even the smallest things.

'After a rather long and disorganised meeting and enrolment session, we all went off and had lunch together. I chatted to Meredith and Amy about their experience on the language course and on their first month in Perugia.

We went out to dinner, before moving on to a bar called Merlin's for drinks and dancing, although no one could out-dance Meredith. This became a regular place to meet up in the evenings, for a drink and a chat. We would speak mostly about our day at university, swapping anecdotes about linguistic mishaps and how we were adapting to life in Italy.

'I would often bump into Meredith around the university, and she would always smile and stop to have a chat. One of my favourite moments occurred on Saturday, 20 October, which was on the night of the rugby World Cup final. We all went to a bar called Shamrocks to watch the game and, despite England losing miserably to South Africa, Meredith did her best to keep our spirits up. She entered into some friendly banter with the guys in front of us, and every time that South Africa scored, she would come out with a witty one-liner. Much hilarity ensued.'

Helen remembers the night of Halloween, only one night before Meredith was murdered, vividly. 'It was the next big social event for us,' she says. 'I got ready at home with my flatmate and the girls from my university, creating makeshift costumes out of bin bags. We had arranged to meet Meredith and the others at Merlin's. By the time our friends turned up, the place was packed and there was barely room to dance. Even the staircase was full of people and Meredith, who had high heels on, was struggling to make her way down it. She was such a petite girl, and I could see at that moment that she would go flying. So I rushed to the bottom of the steps and held out my arms to help her get down. She gave me a big hug to say thanks, and we joined our group of friends.

'After a while chatting, laughing, comparing costumes and taking photographs, we made our way on to the dance floor. It was so busy that we got lost in the crowd, and that was the last time that I saw her.'

Reflecting on that moment, Helen says: 'At the age of twenty, it never crossed my mind that it might have been the last chance to see a friend again. Those first two months were such a wonderful and happy time and, although I didn't know Meredith for very long, I shall never forget her, and I have learnt so much from [her being] such a strong woman ... I make certain that I enjoy and appreciate life and those around me and, most importantly, smile.'

Amy Frost, like Meredith, was studying at Leeds University, but in the two years before going to Perugia she had never met her. 'I think that it was because I was studying French and Italian,' she says, 'and whilst Meredith had already been studying Italian at school for some years, I hadn't, so we were in different classes. Also, I went to France for six months during the second year of my studies, so it was difficult for our paths to cross.

'But before she went to Perugia, Meredith sent emails to the girls she knew would be going there, so that we could connect with each other. I got to Perugia the day before her, and we had arranged to meet at the fountain in the major square in the town centre. By coincidence, I had met Helen Power in the same hotel that I had been staying in, whilst looking for proper accommodation, so I asked her to join us.

'Meredith was late, which I was to learn was a habit of hers. But you could never be angry with her for it. You would arrange a time with her and then add on half an hour. When Meredith arrived at the fountain, I remember thinking how pretty she was, and she was so easy to talk to, with such a good sense of humour. We had such a good time, although we stuck to ourselves quite a bit.'

Robyn Butterworth was also at Leeds University with Meredith, but she was doing a different degree and did not come into contact with her until she arrived in Perugia.

'I'd seen a photograph of Meredith which she had emailed, but it wasn't until I got to Perugia that I saw her for real,' she says. 'Amy Frost and I had agreed to share a place together out there, and we went to a cheap university student café to meet Meredith. She was a bit late, but when she arrived she looked wonderful, and I was surprised at how small she was. She was chirpy and lively from the beginning, and I really liked her.

'When we got to Italy, we thought that everyone was going to be dressed so fashionably, but they weren't. We always dressed quite casually, because we didn't want to be obviously seen to be British. Meredith had quite a lot of shoes, and she loved her boots, which made her seem taller.

'Although Meredith enjoyed socialising, she was quite studious and would often stay at home doing her university work in the evenings. But quite a few times, she would come to our flat for lunch, and often brought a kebab with her, which we found amusing; she loved them.

'Occasionally, we would go to see a British film at the cinema, and the one in Perugia was like an old theatre, a lovely place. I was in some of the same university classes with Meredith, and it always surprised me how she could turn up late and somehow get straight into the lecture and write incredible notes, which she was quite happy to share with me. She was like that, always ready to help people.

'But the afternoon of 1 November was one of the most wonderful I have spent. We all chatted for ages, ate a meal, watched a movie, and it was all so relaxed. When Meredith left with Sophie at about 9 p.m., I never imagined that I would never hear her laugh again.'

Only a few days before, Meredith had been talking to me during our evening phone call about a university trip to Turin and we discussed the possibility that she might be able to see the famous Turin Shroud. Unfortunately, she discovered that the trip was fully booked, and so she was hoping to get on the next one. Meanwhile, I was urging her to go to Venice, if she could find the time. She would never get there.

Sophie Purton was the last one of Meredith's friends to see her alive. She had never met Meredith prior to travelling to Perugia. 'I chose the city because my university department had an affiliation with it,' she says. 'I found somewhere to live with another English girl, who was Amy Frost. She already knew Meredith, and it was through her that I was introduced to her. So, on that first evening, we all went out for a pizza.

'I instantly warmed to Meredith, and she was really amusing; we had a lot of dynamics on that first night. She and Amy were the witty ones, quite alike in some ways, and bounced things off each other. I'd say something stupid and they would make jokes about it, but never in a cruel way. In the evenings, we would sometimes go to the Merlin bar in Via del Forno, a place which was a cross between a pizzeria and a bar. They would have a DJ playing music, and lots of us would dance on the tables.'

Pasquale Alessi, co-owner of Merlin's, has said: 'Meredith was a really nice girl. She liked to go out with her friends. But I never saw her with any problems; never saw her drunk. She always liked to go out with Sophie and Robyn, but she would watch out for them. She was the careful one. "Now we have to go home," she would say, "as we have to get up tomorrow and go to class."'

Another favourite place, according to Sophie, was Tana dell'Orso in Via Ulisse Rocchi. It's a delightful place with a cellar-like feel to its dining room and a garden area with white umbrellas over the tables. 'There were always a lot of Americans there,' says Sophie. 'I don't know why it was so popular with them.' She recalls: 'Daytimes we would go to the main street where there are lots of cafés, and have a coffee or chocolate. Meredith loved her chocolate. There was also a kind of refectory at the University for Foreigners, where you could get cheap lunches, like a bread roll and a bit of fruit for a few euros. I was always amused by her love of kebabs. In England, we tend to go for one after a night out, but it is a different culture in Italy, and I would sometimes find her eating one in the middle of the day.'

On 1 November, Sophie and Meredith went to Amy and Robyn's flat in the late afternoon to watch a DVD of the movie *The Notebook*, and to have pizza and ice cream. Everyone was tired from Halloween the night before, and Meredith said that she had to finish a university assignment. She left with Sophie around nine o'clock and Amy Frost says: 'Meredith said, "See you in the morning at ten o'clock." Then, she came running back and jokingly added: "I mean ten thirty!", meaning that she would probably be late.'

Sophie walked with Meredith back towards the direction of the cottage, leaving her only 500 metres from her front door. There, they said goodbye and went their respective ways.

It was to be the last time that she saw her alive.

4

The Investigation

The weeks following our return from our first trip to Perugia were a distressing time for our family. Not only had we lost a beloved daughter and sister, but we felt far removed from what was happening in the wake of her death, and it was difficult to match one thing to the other. We were, after all, distanced by being in a different country, and all of the developments were unfolding in a different language, so that it felt as if this was all happening in another world. Information was gradually being relayed to us by our lawyer in Florence, Francesco Maresca. Sometimes he would speak on the telephone with Stephanie, who understood Italian, and on other occasions we would talk to him through his interpreter. We were also getting fragmented details on the Internet of events as they unfolded, but these were difficult to trust and we did not know where the truth lay. At this stage, most of the web information we could find came through translations of the Italian media, particularly the newspaper *La Repubblica*. How had Meredith died? How had she been discovered? Who was responsible? These were the questions that our family was debating. Though we lived apart, we spoke to each other every day, if not to keep abreast of new developments, then only so that we could share our utter disbelief that this had happened. At this stage, we didn't realise that Meredith's housemate Amanda Knox and her boyfriend were becoming the police's prime suspects. All we could think of was, who would have done this terrible crime and why? Meredith was the last person in the world that anyone would want to harm. Everyone loved her.

It was not only us and it was not only the people of the small town of Perugia who were in shock, it was all Italians. Murders like this simply did not happen in their country. Sometimes there were murders that were gang-, drug- or vendetta-related, perhaps even the occasional crime passionnel, but not the savage and brutal killing of a British female student – and certainly not in such a peaceful place as Perugia, which, we read, had not seen a killing for more than twenty years.

When I had originally been told by the *Daily Mirror* on 2 November that the British girl's mobile phone had been found, I had no idea where. In our minds it was still like a jigsaw and we were searching for the right pieces to assemble into a coherent picture. As it materialised, this was also the difficulty for the Italian police. Later, we were able to make some sense of how that terrible morning had played out, but for now we were totally oblivious, struck dumb by the fact we would never see or hear from Meredith again.

On that morning of 2 November, as students in Perugia were on their way to their respective universities, at 5b Via Sperandio a drama was about to unfold.

Going into her garden, following a bomb threat to her home that later proved to be a hoax, Mrs Lana Biscarini, who lived only half a mile from Meredith's cottage, found a mobile phone ringing at the bottom of her garden. Curious, she went to investigate and, upon finding it, was baffled. Thinking the hoax call and the mobile might be connected, she immediately telephoned the police, then reportedly took the mobile to her local police station, at their request. There, they ascertained that the mobile belonged to an Italian girl, Filomena Romanelli, who was Meredith's housemate. Soon after, Biscarini's daughter telephoned her mother to say that she had found a second phone in the garden. This, it transpired, belonged to Meredith. The postal police, who are responsible for investigating crimes involving communication technology (including crimes involving the Internet and mobile phones), were dispatched to the cottage where Filomena lived with Meredith in an attempt to solve the mystery.

Chief Inspector Michele Battistelli and Assistant Inspector Fabio Marzi went to the cottage to try to determine why these two mobile phones had been dumped in a garden one kilometre away. Later, they would discover that although the first phone was registered to Filomena, she had actually loaned it to Meredith, in order for her to make cheaper and easier calls within Italy itself. Hence, both phones found dumped at the bottom of the Biscarinis' garden belonged to my daughter.

Meredith, Amanda Knox, Filomena and another Italian girl, Laura Mezzetti, all shared the second floor of the cottage, while the ground floor was shared by four Italian boys: Giacomo Silenzi, Marco Marzan, Stefano Bonassi and Ricardo Luciani. All four Italian boys had been away the previous evening as it was a public holiday, as had Filomena and Laura Mezzetti.

When Battistelli and Marzi arrived at the cottage, they found Amanda Knox and her Italian boyfriend, Raffaele Sollecito, standing outside with a mop and bucket. Later, they testified that the couple looked 'surprised and embarrassed', and were whispering to each other. They told the police they had discovered there had been a break-in at the cottage and that they were waiting for the regular police to arrive. However, Italian police testimony was to indicate that no such call to the police could be proven from telephone records. The call, in fact, was said to have been registered some twenty minutes after the postal police had arrived.

Meredith's housemate Filomena is one of the first people that Amanda Knox is supposed to have called. Filomena had spent the night of 1 November out of town with her boyfriend, Marco Zaroli. On the morning of 2 November, she was back in Perugia, at the Fair of the

Dead, an annual event celebrating both All Saints' Day on 1 November and All Souls' Day on the second, when friends and family gather to remember those who have died. While at the fair, she received a call from Knox, who told her that she had slept at Raffaele Sollecito's place, and that when she had got back to the cottage she had found the front door open and blood in the bathroom. 'She told me that she had taken a shower,' Filomena later said in court, 'and that she was scared and was going to phone Raffaele. It seemed really strange to me, and I asked her to check that the house was in order.'

Knox then telephoned Filomena twice more. Filomena said that on the third call, 'She told me that the window in my room was broken and that my room was in a mess. I told her to call the police and she said that she already had.'

Filomena then rang her friend Luca Altieri and his girl-friend, Paola Grande, to go ahead to the cottage, as they were nearer than she was, saying that she would follow shortly.

When the postal police arrived at the cottage, at around 12.35 p.m., they discovered that a window in Filomena's room had indeed been broken, 'suggesting' the break-in that Knox and Sollecito had told them about. Clothes were scattered across the floor, indicating that the room had been ransacked.

Yet Chief Inspector Battistelli was later to say in court that the glass from the broken window was on top of the clothes. This implied that the clothes had been scattered on the floor first, and that the window had been broken afterwards. It looked to him as if the break-in had been staged. Furthermore, valuables such as jewellery and a laptop were still in the room, making the idea of burglary suspect. When Filomena arrived at the cottage, following Knox's call, already aware that her bedroom window had been broken, she went straight to her room to check it out. 'The room was a disaster,' she said. 'I remember that, in lifting the computer, I realised that I was picking up bits of glass, because the glass was on top.'

The height of the window from the ground led to more questions. Giacinto Profazio, who was at that time head of Perugia's Flying Squad, and who had been called into the investigation, later testified as to the near impossibility of anyone climbing in through the broken window in Filomena's room. 'I thought it strange,' he said, 'as it would have needed a superhuman effort to climb up to it. There was a much easier way into the cottage at the back, via a terrace and a boiler. There was a chair and a table on the terrace, and it would have been a lot easier to get in this way.'

The postal police, along with Filomena, her boyfriend and friends Luca and Paola, entered the cottage to discover that Meredith's bedroom door was locked. Amanda Knox – who, with her boyfriend Sollecito, also came into the cottage – is said to have stated that Meredith often locked her door, something that Filomena would later dispute. Yet the fact remained that Meredith's bedroom

Meredith aged two. She was a beautiful little girl.

Meredith at one and a half, opening Christmas presents.

Meredith aged six, looking
smart in her school uniform
in our garden at home.

Meredith at Keston School aged six.

Meredith was always exceptionally close to her older sister Stephanie.

Meredith and Stephanie playing on a day out at the seaside.

Meredith aged ten.

John, Lyle, me, Stephanie and
Meredith at home in 1991.

Meredith always loved
going to ballet lessons.

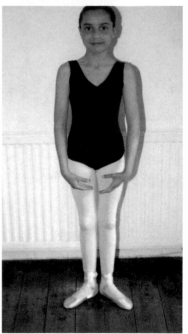

Meredith aged seven.

Arline, Meredith, Stephanie and me in 1992.

Celebrating at Meredith's ninth birthday party.

Meredith, determined to try out her sledge in our garden.

Meredith aged twelve, in costume for a school show.

Meredith on her 21st birthday. Stephanie arranged for a cake to be made with a photo of Meredith aged two printed on top, and she loved it.

Arline, Meredith and
Stephanie with their
grandson and nephew,
Max. Meredith
adored him.

Stephanie and
Meredith at
Stephanie's
Graduation day
in Portsmouth.

Meredith opening her
21st birthday presents.

One of my favourite photos of Meredith and I,
taken when she was fifteen.

door was sealed, and nobody knew where Meredith was. With Knox and Sollecito having retreated to a different room, Chief Inspector Battistelli gave permission for Luca to kick it down. When he did so, the group present were confronted with a scene of blood on the floor and walls.

The scene inside shocked Filomena, her friends and Battistelli. As well as the blood staining the floor and walls, they saw a foot protruding from a duvet that was heaped on the floor.

Battistelli said: 'I looked and, when I saw the scene, I told everyone to get out. There was blood everywhere. That was when I called the operations room.'

What had begun as a curious case of two dumped mobile phones had quickly turned into a murder investigation. It was Meredith who lay underneath the duvet on the floor. Battistelli ordered everybody to leave, sealed the room again, and called for homicide detectives to come.

When the head of Homicide, Monica Napoleone, arrived and saw Meredith's body, she said that she was horrified at the wounds Meredith had on her, especially the savage cut to her throat. There were so many cuts and bruises on Meredith's body, which implied to the police that more than one person had been involved in her killing.

Of course, except for Filomena, Meredith's other friends were completely unaware of this tragic event.

Amy Frost says: 'The second of November was a strange day, because the day before had been a holiday, and we had all been studying all day. Robyn Butterworth, my flatmate, had been ringing Meredith, because she had borrowed a history book from her, which she needed that day, but Meredith was not answering. Robyn was going to walk down to Meredith's house, but didn't.

'None of us had a television, so we didn't see any of the news, but we received a call from a woman at the university office who told us what had happened. She mentioned a girl called Meredith, but she said that the girl was Welsh and twenty-two years old, neither of which fitted the description of our Meredith. The woman told us that she would try to get some more information – but we were worried.

'At this time, we set off for Meredith's cottage to try and get Robyn's book, but Sophie Purton got a phone call from the police telling us all to meet them at the university. They were still saying that the girl was Welsh.

'When we got there, the police arrived and asked us to get into a plain police car. We didn't know where we were going and still didn't know what had happened to Meredith. This was at about six o'clock in the evening. When we arrived at the police station, we were put into a waiting room. That was Robyn, Sophie and me. Then, Meredith's housemate, Laura, walked in. She was crying – and it was then that we realised that it really was the Meredith that we all knew.'

Meanwhile, Amanda Knox's boyfriend, Raffaele Sollecito, had also been called in for questioning, and Amanda had decided to go with him. They were driven to the police station by Filomena's friends Luca and Paola in their car. The couple later alleged that Raffaele was constantly asking them questions regarding the investigation 'in a manner which caused them to be concerned and suspicious'. It was later pointed out on the website, *True Justice for Meredith Kercher*, an unbiased and non-profit-making website, which originated in America and is contributed to by American and Italian lawyers, that after they had dropped Knox and Sollecito off at the police station, Luca and Paola were so concerned they 'thoroughly checked the interior of their car for any incriminating evidence, as they were scared that something might have been planted there'.

At the police station, Meredith's friends were distraught and crying, but it was the behaviour of Knox and Sollecito that attracted the attention of Monica Napoleone and other police personnel.

Napoleone was later to testify that 'Amanda had complained that she was feeling tired and, at one stage, I told her that she could go if she wanted to, but she said that she wanted to stay and wait for Raffaele. A few minutes later, I walked past a room at the police station and I saw Amanda doing the splits and a cartwheel.

'She and Sollecito had had a bizarre attitude throughout the whole time. They seemed completely indifferent to everything. They were lying down, laughing, kissing, pulling faces at each other, and writing notes to each other. They were talking to each other in low voices for the whole time. It was impossible that they were behaving like this when a dead body was in Amanda's house. It seemed strange to everybody.

'When they were brought in after poor Meredith's body had been found, the flatmates and the British friends were very upset, but Knox and Sollecito seemed more interested in each other. They were indifferent to their situation, and I found it quite disturbing, considering that the body of a young girl had been found in such terrible circumstances.'

Inspector Ficarra of the Perugia Flying Squad later said: 'I was in the elevator, and when I got to the floor where the Flying Squad department is, the door opened, and I saw Knox doing floor exercises. She was doing the splits, cartwheels and arching herself backwards, pressing her hands on the floor. I said to her: "What are you doing? Is this the right way to behave?"'

Meredith's friend Robyn Butterworth later recalled: 'I remember how Amanda kept going on about how she had found the body. It was as if she was proud to have been the one who had found it.' And yet those present at the cottage when Meredith's bedroom door was broken down all said that Knox was not within sight of the room. 'I remember thinking that Amanda's behaviour was very strange,' Robyn continued. 'It was as if she wasn't bothered at all . . . When I went into the waiting room, Amanda was talking at the top of her voice in English to everyone there. She described how she had come back to the cottage at 11 a.m. She said that she had found the front door open and that she gone to the bathroom that she and Meredith shared. She was saying how she had seen blood on the floor. She also said that she had taken a shower.'

Filomena had also mentioned Amanda having told her that she had taken a shower, and that she had thought it odd that she would do so in the circumstances, having just found blood on the floor.

Indeed, this was not the first time the girls had found Amanda Knox's behaviour odd. Robyn Butterworth recalled that 'Amanda's behaviour was always a little strange. Even before 2 November, she seemed to be the extravagant type. I remember that the first time we met we were in a restaurant having a meal when, all of a sudden, she got up and started singing at the top of her voice. It was very strange and out of place.'

The prosecutor Giuliano Mignini had accompanied the head of the Homicide Squad, Monica Napoleone, and Meredith's three flatmates, Amanda, Laura and Filomena to the cottage. The investigators wanted the flatmates to check the knives in the kitchen and see if any were missing. As Mignini showed the young women the knives, Amanda suddenly started to sob. She broke down in tears and trembled. It was the first time either Mignini or Napoleoni had seen Amanda in tears.

Under questioning during the next three days, the alibis of Knox and Sollecito kept changing. At first, Amanda claimed to have been at Sollecito's flat all evening on the night of the murder. Then Sollecito claimed that Amanda had left his place at around 9 p.m. and not returned until 1 a.m., during which time he had been on the Internet. Amanda then changed her story to say that she had been at the cottage at the time that Meredith was killed.

Nor were these the only contradictory claims that Knox made while being questioned. As we were later to learn, it was during these first days of questioning that she claimed that Diya 'Patrick' Lumumba, the owner of a local bar, Le Chic, was the murderer. Lumumba, of Congolese origin, had been living legally in Italy since 1988, running the bar where Amanda Knox herself had a part-time job. Police were looking through her mobile phone at the police station, and when they showed her a text she had sent Patrick earlier that evening (having previously denied doing so), she exclaimed: 'Yes, it was him. He did it!' Knox went on to say that 'Patrick and Meredith were in Meredith's room, while I stayed in the kitchen. I can't remember how long they were together in the room, but I can only say that, at a certain point, I heard Meredith screaming and I was so scared, so I covered my ears. After this, I don't remember if Meredith called out or if I heard thuds, because I was upset, but I could imagine what was happening.'

Later, after her arrest, she was to change and embellish this version of events in a written statement to the police: 'I saw Lumumba near the basketball court. I saw him at my front door. I saw myself cowering in the kitchen, with my hands over my ears because, in my head, I could hear Meredith screaming. These things seem unreal to me, like a dream. The truth is that I am unaware of the truth. I know that I didn't kill Meredith. In these flashbacks that

I'm having, I see Patrick as the murderer, but I do not remember for sure if I was at my house that night.'

On hearing Amanda's claim that Patrick Lumumba was the killer, police went to the home he shared with his Polish partner and their eighteen-month-old son on 6 November, and arrested him.

Lumumba was to say later: 'Police came to my home when I was warming some milk for my son. They handcuffed me and only said: "You know what you did." I was not badly treated, but it was a hard situation . . .'

When news of Lumumba's arrest for murder broke, there was shock in many quarters of Perugia. Esteban Pascual, owner of La Tana dell'Orso bar, said: 'I have known him for eight years, and I can't believe it. He worked at the university organising cultural events and concerts and is from a respectable family. He is a nice person. He has never been in any trouble the whole time that I have known him.'

Back in England, this was the first big piece of news we had heard concerning the investigation into Meredith's murder. Pictures of Lumumba were being shown on television, and at our separate family homes we looked on in disbelief, not knowing whether to believe that we were seeing images of the man who had killed our daughter. I spoke with Arline on the telephone, and neither of us could believe that we were looking at the killer. He did not look like a violent man. He was not that tall, had short hair and a slightly plump face. I have never before had to question if I was looking into the eyes of a killer, and it struck me how normal he looked. He appeared to look confused when we saw film footage of him on the television news. I felt anger. Were we looking at the man who had murdered our daughter? Was this really the man who had taken Meredith's life away?

Lumumba told the police that he had never been to the house where Meredith and Amanda lived. 'I only saw Meredith about four times, of which the final time was when she was dressed as a vampire for Halloween. I had told her to come to the bar on the Friday where we could make her special mojitos, that she had previously told me she was good at doing.'

This, at least, seemed to make sense. In one of our evening phone calls, Meredith had told us that she had been to a bar and told the owner that, with her previous bar experience, she could make wonderful mojitos. In fact, she knew how to make about twenty different cocktails.

Lumumba declared to police: 'I was at my bar all of that evening, the first November. When I shut the bar, I went home. I knew Meredith, but I wasn't meeting her. It's not true what Amanda says, that I wanted to be with her. I met Amanda when she was looking for a job and employed her to work twice a week, on a Tuesday and Friday.'

Suspicious of the conflicting stories being told to them by Sollecito and Knox, requests for their arrests as suspects in the murder were made. Until this point, Knox and Sollecito had been regarded as 'witnesses'. Now, the whole thing translated into a far more serious matter. Five days after the horrific killing, Judge Claudia Matteini granted the request for their arrests. Whilst not officially charging them with murder, she said in a leaked report that there was sufficient evidence to hold them, because of the risk that they might flee the country. Lumumba, meanwhile, was already being held.

In her report, Judge Matteini outlined a scenario for the events of the night of 1 November, saying that Meredith had been forced to have sex against her will and had been threatened with a knife, and that the threat had developed into something more serious. It was claimed that Lumumba was the instigator of the sexual attack, but that all three suspects had been involved.

It was at this point that, back in England, things became even more distressing for us. Although we knew that Meredith had been killed as the result of a knife wound to her throat, we had not realised that this action had been preceded by a sexual assault. This was particularly distressing to hear, for it put into a new light what Meredith's final moments must have been like. How could anyone do this to her? we asked ourselves. What was the basis for the attack? Why had she been singled out for this kind of treatment?

It felt as if, with every news report or detail that was coming out of Italy, things were becoming more and more terrible. That Meredith was gone was tragedy enough, but every detail only seemed to worsen what she had been through. A report revealed that the post-mortem on

Meredith, which had been conducted before our first trip to Perugia to identify her body, had revealed bruising on her lips and gums that was consistent with her having been forced into a prone position, as well as with her face being crushed on the ground to hold her still. It also said that there were marks on Meredith's neck, which implied that she had been threatened twice with a knife, before the third cut provided the fatal wound.

The news that Amanda Knox was being held for the murder sent shock waves through our family. I first heard of it via the news and relayed it to Arline, who simply could not comprehend that Meredith's own housemate might have been involved in this terrible crime. 'Amanda? Amanda?' she kept repeating, in a state of utter disbelief. We knew that Meredith had not got on with Knox. Meredith had expressed irritation to both Arline and I and her friends in Perugia at Knox's personal habits, because she frequently failed to flush the toilet and had concerns over how she would 'bring strange men back to the house', but the idea that this irritation could lead to murder seemed preposterous. We knew so little of the American girl and absolutely nothing of her boyfriend, Raffaele Sollecito, a man whom Meredith had never mentioned.

Two weeks later, the chief prosecutor assigned to the case, Giuliano Mignini, asked for Lumumba's release, saying: 'There are no longer any serious indications linking him to the crime. However, he remains under investigation.' There was said to be no proof of his presence at the cottage on the night of the killing. Furthermore, witnesses had vouched that they had seen him in his bar, Le Chic, on the night in question, providing him with a solid alibi.

It was to be two weeks before he would be released for lack of evidence. On regaining his freedom on 20 November, Lumumba had his own ideas as to why he had been arrested for such a terrible crime. 'I believe that Ms Knox had the idea of implicating me when we had met outside the University for Foreigners,' he said. This was three days after the murder and two days before Knox and Sollecito's arrest. Until then, they had both been free to go about their lives as usual, but were being recalled to the police station for further witness statements. 'I had been discussing with one of the university teachers whether I would be a suitable person to act as a translator for reporters from Britain, who did not speak Italian. At this moment, I saw Amanda arriving and I asked her if she liked the idea. She said "No" and went off smiling. Perhaps that was the moment when she decided to land me in it.'

He was also quoted as saying: 'I think that Amanda wanted to derail the investigation. That's what I think. She must have realised that the investigation was leading to her and thought that, if she mentioned me, then the investigators' attention would shift to me. I can tell you that she wants to be the centre of attention. I think that she is a person capable of doing anything to be in the spotlight.'

He was further quoted as saying: 'Amanda hated Meredith, because people loved her more than Amanda. She was insanely jealous that Meredith was taking over her position as Queen Bee.'

Trying to come to terms with the nightmare of Meredith's murder in the few days following her death was one thing – we had assumed that a random killer had broken into her room – but nothing had prepared us for the shock that Amanda Knox and her boyfriend were now suspects.

The news of Amanda's arrest had set the world's media alight, and they were now beginning to build a profile of her. One British newspaper, the *Daily Mail*, had already dubbed her 'Foxy Knoxy', a name that would come to define the case and shift its focus entirely from Meredith and the other suspects. As a family, we were not pleased that she had been given this title, as it seemed a some-what cosy name and did not reflect the horror of the events.

Reeling from the shock of these developments, we tried to get our bearings by finding out more about Amanda Knox. I read in newspapers and on the Internet that Knox was born in Seattle, the daughter of Curt Knox, then a retail executive, and his wife, Edda, a primary school teacher. Amanda's sister, Deanna, was born a year later. After only a few years, Amanda's parents divorced and Amanda went to Seattle Preparatory School, described as a strict Jesuit institution. Her mother, Edda, married Christopher Mellas, who at the time was only twenty-seven years old.

Amanda later went to the University of Washington to study English, German and Italian.

She had always been considered studious but, according to some students, she led a 'double life'. Whilst some saw her as being academically conscientious, others portrayed her quite differently. One of her contemporaries, talking to the *Daily Mail*, said: 'We all liked to smoke a bit of pot, and go out and get trashed at weekends, but she really used drink and drugs. By that, I mean that she didn't simply take stuff to get high and have fun. It was like she wanted to get away from herself, as if she had some chemical imbalance she could only cope with by getting wasted.'

In 2006, she rented a place away from the university campus and, a few months before she left for Italy, she was given a criminal conviction and fined $269 for being at an unruly party where, it was reported, rocks were thrown at passing cars.

After her arrest, Clint Van Zandt, who had been a long-serving employee of the FBI's Behavioral Science Unit, told NBC News's Dennis Murphy: 'Realise that this is a woman wearing two masks. One mask is Amanda the good girl, in a Catholic school, an athlete, does what her mother says. And then you've got the other mask that, when she gets to Italy, it's "I'm going wild. I'm having fun. This is where I sow my wild oats." Now, which is the true Amanda? Probably both'.

Raffaele Sollecito, meanwhile, remained a somewhat quiet figure in the background. He looked, to me, like a typical bespectacled student. At the time of his arrest, he was twenty-three years old, three years older than Amanda. The son of a prominent urologist, Francesco Sollecito from Giovinazzo in southern Italy, he had led a privileged life. School friends have described him as quiet and studious. Yet he described himself on a social networking site as being 'sweet, but sometimes absolutely crazy'. He even appeared in pictures posted on the Internet wielding a meat cleaver. He was studying computer science at the University of Perugia when he met Amanda Knox, two weeks before Meredith was murdered.

Things became more sinister when police disclosed that he always carried a knife with him, and that he was passionate about collecting knives. After the murder, police were prompted to search his flat and discovered a collection of Japanese manga comics, some of which depicted acts of extreme violence. One, which attracted particular attention, was concerned with the killing of female vampires on Halloween. It was not lost on police that Meredith had been dressed as a vampire to celebrate Halloween only one night before she was murdered, and they later went on to say that the scene they discovered at the cottage was reminiscent of the scenes depicted in Sollecito's comics. Upon learning this, we could not help but wonder if Meredith's murder had been premeditated, even though the cases that would later be put forward all suggested that it had been a spontaneous act.

In England, we were still trying to unravel what was going on in Italy, with only loose information coming through to us. It seemed that every time we thought we were beginning to piece together the facts of what had happened, something else would emerge. We had only just come to terms with the fact that Diya 'Patrick' Lumumba was the prime suspect, but no sooner had we found some way to cope with that realisation, than we learned that Lumumba was being released while Knox and Sollecito remained under arrest. So far away from the investigation, we were lost.

A short while before Patrick Lumumba was released, the investigation took another alarming turn. The police identified a bloodied fingerprint on Meredith's pillow that did not match any of the three suspects currently being investigated. A fourth person, it seemed, had now entered the scene of the investigation.

Having run the newly discovered fingerprint through their computers, the police ascertained that it belonged to one Rudy Hermann Guede, an immigrant from the Ivory Coast who had already been arrested for petty theft and drug dealing. They immediately searched his flat and took DNA samples from his toothbrush, which later proved to match DNA found on and inside Meredith's body. This seemed to tie Guede, without doubt, to the scene of Meredith's murder – but it was not the only evidence placing him at the cottage that night. Previous information from members of the public had already provided police with details of a man of African origin fleeing the cottage on the night of the murder, later to be seen washing clothes in a launderette.

Guede had arrived in Italy from the Ivory Coast in Africa in 1992, at five years of age, with his father. When Guede was fifteen, his father had returned to Africa and he had been left in the care of a wealthy Italian, Paolo Caporali, for whom he had done occasional work.

Caporali was later to say: 'We gave him an opportunity, even though we knew that he was a liar, but we wanted to give him a chance. We took him in as a son, but he was interested in other things than studying and work. We gave him a job, but we had to sack him because he was never there. In the end, we asked him to leave our home, because we couldn't cope any longer and we have had no contact with him since. I thought that I could help him build a future, but I realised that I had made a mistake. He was a tremendous liar, saying that he had been to school, when he had skipped lessons and watched television and played video games all day.'

Meanwhile, one of the Italian male students who lived in the flat below Meredith told police in a statement: 'One guy who came to our home was tall and thin, and he always wore basketball shoes and baggy trousers. He was nicknamed "Body Raga".' Rudy Guede was known to be a fervent basketball player.

However, Guede could not be found in Perugia, and it seemed as if nobody knew where he had fled. Some people reported that they had seen him on the night of Meredith's murder, dancing in a Perugian club, and others told police that he said he was going to go dancing in Milan. That he did indeed go to Milan seems probable, but efforts by Italian police to locate him were, at this time, fruitless. Indeed, there seemed little hope of quickly locating Guede until one of his friends, Giacomo Benedetti, went to the police and told them that Guede had contacted him by email and was in Germany.

Knowing this, police set out to try to lure Guede back to Italy. Having made contact by posing as a friend on Facebook, they fed questions to Guede, hoping to pinpoint his location and tempt him back on to Italian territory. The following is an alleged transcript of that 'conversation', which was later reproduced on the website True Justice for Meredith Kercher:

Friend: *Hi, Rudy. How are you?*
Rudy: *Not too well.*
Friend: *Where are you?*
Rudy: *I'm in Dusseldorf. I have no money. I'm living on a barge and sleeping on trains without paying for a ticket. It's tough. I can't do this any more.*
Friend: *Would you like me to send you some money?*
Rudy: *That would be useful.*
Friend: *I'll send you 50 euros through Western Union, then you can pick it up.*
Rudy: *Thanks, but it's already late in the evening.*
Friend: *They're talking about you here.*
Rudy: *I know what happened in Perugia, but they are making a mistake.*

Friend: *But they are saying other things.*

Rudy: *Listen, you know that I knew those girls,*
Meredith and Amanda, but nothing more. You
know that I've been to their house twice; the
last time a few days before all of this business. I
wasn't there that evening. If they have found my
fingerprints, it means I must have left them there
before.

Friend: *But your photo is everywhere.*

Rudy: *I've seen it. The police were wrong to put my*
photo around like that. I'm not how they describe
me. I have nothing to do with that night.

Friend: *But if you have nothing to do with it, why*
don't you come back? I'll help you find a good
lawyer who can clear things up.

Rudy: *I'm afraid. But I don't want to stay in*
Germany. I'm black, and if the police catch me,
I don't know what they might do to me. I prefer
Italian jails.

Rudy was presumably not telling his 'friend' all the facts. When he said that the fingerprint discovered at the cottage must have been left there from a previous visit, he was obviously unaware that it had been a bloodied one that placed him at the scene of the crime. The forensic examination of his DNA would also place him there.

Playing on Rudy's fear of not wanting to stay in Germany or be arrested in that country, the Italian police offered to wire him fifty euros via Western Union. They even worked out the trains and times for him to travel to Milan. It seemed that Rudy might have agreed to this plan, hoping to sneak back into Italy.

Giacinto Profazio of the Perugian Flying Squad said: 'It was a brilliant operation. We'd known for several days that he was in Germany. We contacted him via Facebook. An officer pretended to be a friend of his and convinced him to return to Italy.'

Profazio then sent police, headed by the chief of Homicide, Monica Napoleone, to arrest him as he crossed the border into Italy. Yet somehow, Rudy did not arrive.

Instead, he was on a train travelling towards the German city of Mainz when a train inspector detained him for not having a ticket. Police were informed, and they quickly discovered that he was wanted by the Italian police, who had issued an international arrest warrant for him. Guede was then taken into custody while his extradition was discussed.

Awaiting extradition in a German prison, Guede seems to have changed his story, admitting to police that he was at the cottage on the night of the murder, and insisting that he had gone there for a date with Meredith. As a family, when we read about this, we found it hard to believe, since Meredith would never have behaved this way with a stranger. Guede is said to have told police in Germany that on the night of Meredith's murder, he had gone to the bathroom and while there heard Meredith scream-ing. Emerging from the bathroom, he claimed to have seen an Italian man, whom he first claimed not to have known, wielding a knife, next to Meredith. At this point, he claimed, Meredith was already dying. Meanwhile he claimed that another person, somebody he could neither see nor identify, stood outside the cottage.

Several days later, Guede was extradited to Italy, arriving under police guard at Rome's Fiumicino airport. Here, he was met by Italian police and driven to Perugia's Capanne prison, where he was placed in solitary confinement. Once there, he was to be interviewed by the investigating magistrate, Claudia Matteini, who had been responsible for signing the arrest warrants of the other three suspects. The public prosecutor, Giuliano Mignini, and investigators from Perugia's Flying Squad would also be present.

Guede was later to embark on a new alibi, embellishing his version of events. He was ready to implicate, it seemed, Amanda Knox and Raffaele Sollecito. He claimed that the Italian man with the knife was Sollecito, and that the person outside the cottage was Knox, whose voice he had recognised.

It was the DNA found on and in Meredith's body that convinced Italian police of Guede's complicity in her killing. However, Guede's lawyer at the time, Vittorio Lombardo, was quoted as saying: 'We know about the DNA, but our position has not changed. We have always said that Guede was at the house that night and he has admitted it himself. It is clear that the police will find his DNA there, on the bags and elsewhere. But it does not mean that he is the killer.'

A further legal representative for Guede, Walter Biscotti, talking to Italian journalist Enrico Montana on Italian television five weeks after the murder, said: 'Rudy saw a man coming out of Meredith's bedroom, who was smaller than him. There was a struggle. The man said to him in Italian: "You are a black man. You'll get the blame." Guede was in a very difficult situation. But he did get a towel and try to stop the blood from Meredith's wound before leaving.'

Guede himself was quoted as saying: 'If I had been a man I would have stayed and tried to save Meredith.'

With Lumumba exonerated, the investigation would now centre on Knox, Sollecito and Guede.

All these events had been slowly unfolding as we waited in England for the return of Meredith's body, so that we could organise a funeral and lay her peacefully to rest. We had been relieved to be told that a second autopsy would not be necessary, but it was still almost four weeks before she was flown home. Both Christmas and Meredith's twenty-second birthday were on the horizon, but instead we would be laying her to rest. We hoped that when she arrived in England, it would not be in a simple, nondescript box. As it transpired, the Italians had done her proud, and her body lay in a beautiful polished wood coffin.

It was taken to Rowland Brothers, the funeral directors we had chosen in Coulsdon, whose funeral parlour, ironically, is almost opposite the church where Meredith and Stephanie both been christened as babies. Once she had arrived, Arline and Stephanie went in once more to see her. They seemed pleased, although obviously upset, that they had one more chance to meet with her. Again, I could not face the prospect of seeing her like that. In my mind, she was still alive, like she still is today: on her way to work or meet friends, or to see us her family, probably running late, full of news and eagerness at what the day holds in store.

5

The Funeral

Meredith was at the funeral parlour of Rowland Brothers for two weeks after she had been returned from Perugia in that beautiful, polished wood coffin. There was still some discussion in Italy by the defence lawyers for Knox, Sollecito and Guede as to whether her body would have to be returned from England for a further autopsy. It was an agonising time for our family. Having waited so long for her to come to us and worrying whether a second autopsy would be demanded, the last thing we wanted was to have to delay her funeral further. Finally, in December we received the news that no further autopsy was required, and we were able to lay Meredith to rest.

On the morning of 14 December, the day of her funeral, and only two weeks before what would have been her twenty-second birthday, our family gathered at the funeral parlour. I looked across the road to St John's Parish Church, which dates from 1269. It was a poignant moment for me, because I could still remember her christening and the vicar holding Meredith over the font. It was so sad that I was now looking towards the church for entirely different reasons.

We climbed into limousines behind the hearse, looking at the flowers in its back window, along with photographs that had been contributed by Meredith's friends, which was a lovely touch. There was also a floral tribute from the city of Perugia. I thought of the tokens we had asked to be placed in her coffin: her favourite rainbow dress, which Arline and Stephanie had chosen; an Everton football scarf from her brother Lyle; a CD he had compiled of some of her favourite songs, and a letter and message from me. In it, I told her that I loved her and always would.

The cortège moved slowly down the long hill of Coulsdon Road, on its five-mile journey, passing the house where she had spent the first eleven years of her life, and on towards Croydon Parish Church in Croydon's old town. The church is linked to the Old Palace School, where Meredith had studied. We had hardly ever been in the church before, except for Christmas carol services held by the Old Palace School, and I was surprised by its vastness.

As the cortège reached the church, we were the last to arrive; press photographers and film crews were lined up opposite. I had anticipated that there would be approximately 150 people inside the church, and was stunned, as we entered, to find more than 500. Practically everyone who had ever known Meredith was present, and there were also many strangers who wished to pay their respects, having read of the date of the funeral. Friends of Meredith had travelled from Canada, Japan and Europe, an incredible tribute to her. Everyone was holding a programme of the order of the service, which had the words '*A Celebration of the Life of Meredith Susanna Cara Kercher*' printed on the front, and there was a beautiful photograph of her on it too.

There were so many floral tributes that it was obvious they would never be able to be carried on the hearse as it made its way to the cemetery after the ceremony.

Before the service began, the Reverend Colin Boswell, the vicar of Croydon, who is also chaplain to the Old Palace School, said that the service would 'hopefully bring some life and light into what is a very dark situation.' He added: 'A life should not be judged on its length, but on its quality and the love which surrounded it.'

As he began his sermon, there was great solemnity. 'At all the important moments in our lives, and usually this means a moment of change, there are elements which are important from the past. That is to say, that which has been shared, memories and histories, things that are important for this moment, the present, and things which call us to consider that which is to be. That is to say, the future.

'There is no real ending of course today, but this is at least a moment when some of the waiting can come to an end. It is a long time since the awful moments of the first knowledge of this terrible tragedy have been taken into your consciousness, and these days have not been easy as you have endured news reports, speculation and waiting. Firstly, for Meredith to come home to England, and then to be able to hold this ceremony of thanksgiving, so that you can properly articulate your feelings for her, and allow your own feelings to find their expression inwardly and outwardly, privately in your own heart, among others.

'This is indeed a terrible thing, to gather, in order to thank God for this life, beautiful and loved and loving, which has been so cruelly taken from you; so much that might have been, so many moments of joy and love, that perhaps would have been experienced, but now won't.

'It is those good things that we want to keep in our minds, just like the picture of Meredith on the front of this order of service. That's how we want to remember her, full of life and happiness, for that is how she lived her life and, however brief that life, it is not as if it hasn't been lived. It has made its mark on each of us, and on the world; supremely, of course, her family, and you who once shared the real joy of having her amongst you, and part of you. You remember her and keep her memory alive in your own lives.

'Those of you who are friends will, even from this place of grief, be able to remember her with joy, and with some laughter, as you share together what made her important to you, what you held in common.

'The things that we have heard about her life, and the way that she lived it, these can't be taken from us; this is always going to be a part of us, and I want to encourage you to speak about Meredith. You probably have before the service, and I hope that you are going to afterwards, share stories and memories, because today won't then only be about sadness and loss, it will also be about the joy of friendship and of family love.

'When someone young dies, it is out of place and out of time and, in Meredith's case, it was an act of wickedness and brutality. When one human being loses all their sense of the respect and care and honour that they should have for another, then the whole world suffers as a result of such a dreadful action. But, however painful it is that we shall not have Meredith amongst us in a physical way any more, we live by sight, by touch, and it is difficult when these things are taken from us. However, I believe that Meredith will find her potential as a human being, not in this world, but in a new kind of living, which is beyond the physical.

'I believe that she is now held in love, which is the closer presence of God. I simply couldn't believe that all that was good and creative and loving and lovely about her can be blotted out by even such a terrible death, that all that simply ceases to exist. I cannot believe that all of these things about her are simply no more. Essentially, Meredith is still herself; even more herself.

'When faced with something that is evil and results in death, we must have the courage to stand up and say that death is not the last word. Love is the last word, and always will be, for the meaning is love.

'Meredith, I believe, now understands what that means. She understands a more perfect harmony, deeper colours. She understands the mystery of life, albeit paradoxically through her death. For her, there is now only love.'

Our family, and Meredith's friends, many of whom were in tears, thought that Colin Boswell's speech was particularly moving. It captured the essence of Meredith's personality and touched the thoughts and feelings of everyone present.

Lyle then addressed the congregation, and introduced a respectful tone of levity into his speech, to remind people of Meredith's humour. Referring to her nickname of Mez, which was used on our family's floral tribute, he said: 'She would probably be looking down smiling at that name in flowers, as it reduced the cost of putting her full name.' There were quite a few smiles and laughs as her friends realised that that is precisely what she would have been thinking.

'Mez was notorious for her bad timekeeping. You could set your watch by her, granted that she would always be twenty minutes late. She had a warm and bubbly personality. All of her friends and family can look back and remember her for her endearing qualities, such as her quick wit and fantastic sense of humour.'

The mood of those present was shifting back and forth between grief and smiles and deep thought. Meredith's other brother, John, also read a tribute, recalling what a wonderful girl Meredith was, and also gave a reading from the Book of Revelation, which includes the words:

'To live now in the heart is to never die at all.' Stephanie, meanwhile, had composed a poem for her, 'Don't Say Goodbye', which she read. It is particularly moving and still brings a tear to my eyes when I read it.

Don't be sad, please don't cry,
Don't ask what if, or reason why.
Just remember I love you so,
And this I promise you'll always know.

When you can no longer hear me,
I'll be the wind whisp'ring in your ear.
When you can no longer feel me,
I'll be the sun that holds you near.

When the tears run down your cheeks,
My tears join yours, as raindrops fall.
And when you feel your heart breaking,
Feel mine break too, as stormy skies will call.

When you can see only darkness,
Look to the sparkling stars and moon,
For I will light the darkest skies,
And you and I will be home soon.

When you're feeling lost and helpless,
The ground, a pathless quilt of snow.
I'll be the footprints next to yours,
And hold your hand, a hand you know.

Remember you are never alone,
I am always with you, when you roam.
So close your eyes, I'm with you still.
I haven't left you, I never will.

It is a beautiful poem from one sister to another, and I know that Stephanie meant every word of it.

At this point during the service, a curious thing happened. In my mind I spoke to Meredith and said: 'If you are with us today, can you give us some kind of sign?' Beside the pulpit there was a huge vase of flowers. At this moment, it suddenly toppled over and crashed to the floor. Perhaps it was a coincidence, but I like to think that it wasn't. Perhaps it was unstable where it was perched, but, even so, my eyebrows raised at the timing. It seemed somewhat mischievous, and not the kind of thing that Meredith would have done. Although Meredith could be a bit mischievous at times, she was always very respectful and I don't think she would have done anything disruptive during a church service.

Following Stephanie's reading of her poem, the Old Palace School choir sang the requiem, *'In paradisum'* and then the congregation sang 'For the Beauty of God' and 'Abide with Me'. It was then that one of Meredith's favourite songs by the group U2 was played, 'With or Without You', long and haunting.

After the service, everyone filed out of the church and the Reverend Boswell later remarked: 'It was very moving, but there was some laughter as her brother, Lyle, spoke about things from her life that were not sad.

'It is important, at a funeral like this, that we try to remember things that are happy and good, or else only evil and not very creative things take over, and we have got to try and rise above that.'

As the cortège left the church, heading towards the cemetery in Croydon, I could not help noticing that on one bunch of white roses was the message: '*What a tragic waste. May your smile be as infectious in Heaven as it was on Earth, Mez.*'

Our family had expected, as is usual, for there to be us and a few friends at the cemetery, and were stunned to find around fifty cars lined up and more than 150 people with flowers gathered at the graveside. It was an emotional moment. The assistant curate from Old Palace School, Sarah Goucher, read a tribute, and Meredith's coffin was lowered into the ground. I shall never forget that scene. Once Meredith was in the ground, almost everyone there threw a handful of soil on to the coffin. Dozens of bunches of flowers were laid, with touching and loving messages.

Even the reception, an hour later, was a surprise. The Old Palace School had insisted on hosting it, expecting about fifty people to attend. In the end, almost 200 arrived, cramming into the school library to share their memories of Meredith. Some of her friends from Leeds had brought a photo album with them, to remind us of the happy and amusing times that they had enjoyed together.

One girl, Rowena, who had been a close friend during Meredith's time at Old Palace School, said: 'There are so many memories, some that are still really strong, and others that, to my dismay, are beginning to fade. I hope that my shockingly bad memory can do justice to her, and the friendship that we had.

'Sometimes, while details escape me, the emotions of a memory still hold strong, and all of these memories are positive, of laughter, fun and good times. The locations vary a lot through the years, from Croydon and our meeting up, to working on the tour buses in London together. There are so many ways that we shared our lives, and I'll try to touch on as many as I can.

'Most memories involve our mutual friends, Noita and Kayleigh. So I guess the best place to start is the Japanese restaurant, Miso, in Croydon, which we frequented a lot. We called ourselves the Miso Crew, because we went there so often together, and we have yet to go back there, knowing that you won't be joining us any more.

'We almost always ordered the same meal for ourselves. Meredith's was always a sixty-two on the menu and mine was a Sha Cha Chicken Special. The things that people can see as mundane, like always ordering the same thing on the menu, formed the core glue of our friendship as a group. Not to mention the individual relationships that existed within.

'There were countless trips to Miso, followed by cocktails at the Mexican restaurant, Conchitas, where Meredith often worked at weekends. Once, Meredith even went behind the bar and made the cocktails herself. She was good at that.

'We would sit and talk about everything and anything, quite often about boyfriend trouble, act the fool, take random photographs of each other, while keeping up to date on each other's lives and giving advice when needed. Even when we had to go our separate ways for a while, as when Noita went to America, we always came back together, and that's why our band of four was so strong. In fact, the one time that I went to Miso with none of the others there, it felt so strange that I never did it again.'

Chris Ansell was a long-standing boyfriend of Meredith's when they were in their mid-teens. He has since worked as an English teacher in Thailand. Speaking of the relationship they enjoyed for a year, he said: 'When we were coming to the end of our schooldays, at about sixteen or seventeen years old, we started to go to house parties quite regularly in the summer holidays, and it was at one of these that I first saw her. She was so naturally beautiful, and the first couple of times that we were at the same party, I shied away. But the following week, there was another party and, being summer, it was held in the garden.

'It was under a gazebo, right next to the stereo system, that we first briefly spoke, or rather shouted to each other. I was infatuated with her after that fifteen-minute talk, which prematurely ended when her sister, Stephanie, came to collect her in her little yellow Fiat.

'A couple of weeks later, my parents were away on holiday, and so I decided, or rather my friends decided for me, that I should have a house party. The summer holidays were coming to an end, and it would be the last chance for a while. I made certain, through a friend, that Mez got news of the party. We spoke to each other for a lot longer that night, and kissed for the first time on the garden bench. I felt on top of the world.

'Our first date was a while later. I met her at the station and we went for a long walk. I felt so proud walking with her, and wanted everyone to see. We talked about my gap-year plans and her last year at Old Palace School. She was due to go on a school trip to Italy that year, for two weeks, and she was really excited about it.

'I remember thinking, Wow, this girl knows what she wants and is passionate about it. The trip to Italy that she was going to be taking was months away, and I remember thinking that if we were still together at that time, then those two weeks that she would be away were going to be the longest in my life.

'We walked back home, joking about what an odd first date it had been and that only old people go "for walks". Our early time as a couple was quite intense, and I wouldn't change any of it. Any evenings when we couldn't see each other, we still managed to steal a few hours on the telephone. Our families used to call out to us: "Are you still on the phone?! What else have you got left to talk about?"

'A couple of months later, it was my eighteenth birthday, and we had a big family party at our house. Mez obviously came and I couldn't believe how beautiful she looked in a beige skirt and black top. I was so proud to introduce her to my family. It must have been quite daunting for her, as my extended family is quite large. But she was great, simply being herself.

'There is another lovely memory that I have of an evening out which turned into a very cold, long night. We had decided to go down to the coastal town of Brighton for some food, drinks and a stroll along the beach. It must have been dark quite early; somewhere around winter, as it was absolutely freezing. We lost track of time and missed the last train home. I loved every second that I was with Mez, and so saw this less as a negative and more as a blessing. It was too late to ring for a lift home and so we decided to sit in one of the all-night cafés on the seafront.

'We spent about four hours in there, drinking coffee and hot chocolate until we could get a train home. The walk to the station was probably the coldest that I have ever been and the same, I imagine, for Mez. The train ride was the best of my life. We fell asleep and probably still would have been for weeks if we hadn't woken up at our station, where Meredith's dad collected us and drove us home.'

I remember arriving at the station and seeing them huddled together. It was cold and dark and they seemed pleased to see me arrive in the car.

Chris recalls another train incident that had him laughing. 'We had got a train back from somewhere and, when we arrived, we both got out of different doors. Mez came running up to me and jumped up, wrapping both of her legs and arms around me, only for her jeans to split down the middle seam. The ripping sound was hilarious, and when I saw that the rip was straight down the back of her jeans, I couldn't stop laughing.

'The following summer, we booked a week's holiday in Lanzarote in the Canary Islands, a week on a black rock in the sunshine. The time flew by. We were on the beach by day and eating and drinking by night.

'I guess we wouldn't have been a normal couple without the occasional argument, and Mez had some fairly strong attitudes and opinions, which she would stand up for in any circumstance. In an argument, this was something that I didn't like, because I knew that the odds were stacked against me. But this was also one of the traits which made her such a lovable human being.

'A few months later, I set off on my travels to Fiji and New Zealand, and it was whilst I was there that we split up. She was a beautiful girl in her final year at school, meeting lots of people, whilst I was on the other side of the world also meeting lots of people. I think that because of that, there was a bit of jealousy from both of us, and we broke up.

'It wasn't until we were both at Leeds University, some years later, that we spoke again, and decided to forget what had happened. We bumped into each other on campus on a couple of occasions, and eventually decided to go to a café. I remember standing outside my house so that she could see me, and when she appeared and walked towards me, I can honestly say that I have never seen a more beautiful girl in my life. She was stunning, and the proud feeling I always had when I was with her immediately returned.

'We had lunch, and she told me how much she was looking forward to spending a year in Italy. She was excited about improving her grasp of the language, which she was already good at, and simply leading the life that Italians did.

'She was always incredibly focused, and generally achieved what she set out to achieve. Mez was as happy as I had ever seen her. She never had a problem, wherever she was, with making friends with people. She really was popular, and didn't have to pretend to be someone else to achieve this. We had planned to meet at the Christmas of 2007 when she came back from Italy for the holiday period. But, tragically, it never materialised.

'We experienced a lot of new things together, and I'll always feel so fortunate about that. I would happily have spent my whole life with her, either in a relationship, or as a friend, and feel destroyed that this is no longer possible.'

Speaking with Chris and so many of Meredith's other friends at the reception following the funeral was a moving experience. We had buried my beautiful girl and yet talking about her made her seem so alive. I was grateful to her friends for reliving their memories of her, and sharing laughs as they remembered the funny things she had done and the adventures they had had together.

When everyone had eventually dispersed, we decided, as a family, to have an hour or so together. Our family members all lived in different directions, so we thought that rather than go back to Arline's house, we would adjourn to a country inn a few miles away, where we could be alone and talk about the day's events. We also knew that there would probably be members of the press waiting at the house too, and this would be too much to bear before we had had a chance to chat amongst ourselves.

So we drove to the inn in our separate cars, met up, ordered a bottle of wine and then toasted Meredith, as we would do so many times in the years to follow.

It is so difficult at a time like this to know how to react. We had waited six long weeks for the day when we could finally lay Meredith to rest, and, in some way, I felt a huge relief that, at last, we knew where she was. And, thinking of all the messages and bouquets at the cemetery, I could only hope that she was in a much better place.

We sat quietly at first, replaying the day in our minds. Then, slowly, we started talking about the people who had attended the church. We were amazed at how many people had been there, some we had not seen for years – Meredith and Stephanie's ballet and gymnastics teachers; friends from her school – as well as strangers who had wanted to pay their own tributes. Yet, even though Meredith was now at peace, we were also distinctly aware that this was only the beginning. On the other side of Europe, the investigation continued, with the three people accused of Meredith's murder still in custody, and we were in total confusion at what was happening. There we were, more than 1,500 miles away, dealing with a situation in a language that we were not familiar with. Our only avenue of communication about how things were unfolding in Perugia was through our lawyer, Francesco Maresca, and – excellent as he was – even that was not a simple situation, as he was based in Florence, some two hours from Perugia.

We had no idea when we would next be required to fly to Italy. We were given to understand that the investigation would continue with the further gathering of evidence from the scene of the crime by the Perugian police and forensic experts brought in from Rome, headed by the internationally respected Patrizia Stefanoni. At some point in the New Year, all the evidence would be presented at what, in Italy, is known as a 'pretrial'. Though we had no idea exactly when the pretrial might be held, we knew we might have to be prepared for a long wait.

Yet, as keen as we were to know the truth behind the night of 1 November, in this particular moment we held on to what Meredith had been, and still was, to each and every one of us, looking back over the events of the funeral and knowing that for her family, and all of the friends who had turned out to celebrate her life, Meredith would be remembered for ever.

6

Suspects

For my family and me, 2008 was a time of great uncertainty, and the way in which Meredith had been taken from us left us still feeling raw. We knew that Knox, Sollecito and Guede were being held as suspects, but they had not yet been sent for trial, and thousands of questions buzzed in our minds. That we might not know what had happened to Meredith on her final night for many long months, if ever, was a source of constant pain.

While more evidence was being compiled by the prosecution, a particularly disturbing event occurred in April. We learned that police video footage of Meredith's body had been shown on the Italian television station Telenorba 7, a private television network based in Bari, near to where Raffaele Sollecito comes from. Our lawyer told us of this broadcast and we were shocked that anyone could do something like this.

Richard Owen of *The Times* reported that it showed 'police scientists in white protective clothing pulling back the duvet in Meredith's bedroom to reveal her body and slashed throat, and then turning the corpse over to examine her bloodied back.'

We felt that it was a disgusting abuse of journalistic licence and it was condemned by the Italian Union of Journalists, who said that the station's conduct was unethical. The pictures were originally recorded by forensic police as they collected evidence in the room in the cottage. The footage found its way online, and I can only thank God that we did not stumble across it.

Our lawyer, Francesco Maresca, said: 'The Kercher family are very shocked and distressed. I can't believe that a television station had broadcast such images. This is not a spectacle for entertainment and the people involved should be ashamed. This is an example of gross journalistic misconduct, which evidently violates all of the rules of how to report a story.'

We wholeheartedly agreed with what he said as our representative in Italy, because these were precisely our feelings.

The editor of the Telenorba programme, Enzo Magistra, said: 'When I decided to transmit the images of Meredith's corpse, I did not have the least intention of violating anyone's dignity, but merely to do my job with respect to an important event.'

Listening to this defence only left us more upset. I wondered how the editor of the Telenorba programme might have felt if it was his daughter who had been murdered, and pictures of whose body were now being broadcast without her family's permission? I could not believe that, in similar circumstances, he would have allowed such a public viewing of such an event.

Yet Telenorba were not the only ones seeking to win viewers by exploiting Meredith's death. Later, the film footage was picked up by the Italian state broadcaster RAI, who rebroadcast it.

Anna Maria Ferretti, director of the television programme *Antenna Sud*, was reported in the Italian press as saying: 'For five minutes of television, the ultimate taboo has been broken without any shame.'

Police later alleged that having legally obtained the footage, the Sollecito family had then illegally passed it on to Telenorba.

The fact that Knox, Sollecito and Guede were to be tried in Italy also gave rise to added complications, and we would have to attune ourselves to the way in which the Italian justice system worked. The case was now at the stage in the Italian legal process known as the pretrial. This does not involve a jury, only a judge, who has to evaluate all the evidence presented by the prosecution and the arguments from the defence lawyers, and whose job it is to decide whether or not the suspects should stand trial.

Before the pretrial commenced, the judge was faced with having to read through 10,000 pages of documents. We had no idea how long this process would take, or whether our presence would be required at the commencement of the pretrial, and so we limped on in a sort of limbo, unable to find answers to any of our questions.

We were still so close to Meredith's passing and her absence dominated our thoughts. It was not easy to do any work, but somehow we all managed to, although we spent many evenings together, debating on the telephone about how things could possibly progress. Alone in my flat, I would sit in the living room thinking of her, what she would have been doing if she had still lived, her laugh, her extraordinary wit. Even in my sadness, I would smile at my memories of her. I found myself certain that she was about to call me, as if our routine of daily telephone conversations had never stopped, even though I knew that this was never going to be. I even thought of phoning her, which might seem ridiculous, but it was a thought that kept on going through my mind.

The months passed by slowly, taking us further and further away from the moment Meredith had been murdered. We reached the anniversary of the day she had left England to start her new life in Perugia, and soon afterwards we were told that the pretrial was set to commence, and were asked to travel again to Perugia on 15 September to attend the one-day preliminaries of the pretrial the following day. John and Lyle were unable to make the date due to work commitments, and the cost of our fares, but Stephanie, Arline and I agreed to go.

Whereas the first time we had gone to Italy we had flown to Florence and been met by members of the British Consulate there, this time our lawyer Francesco Maresca arranged for us to fly to Rome. Of course, since we had no financial help from the Foreign Office, we had to fund our trip ourselves. On our arrival, a small contingent of press photographers was waiting for us. In the airport, we were met by police, including the head of Perugia's Homicide Squad, Monica Napoleone, a good-looking and stylish middle-aged lady whom we had only briefly met before. Her dark black hair framed a hard, tanned face, but her smile was welcoming.

The people at the airport did not seem to take that much notice of us as we climbed into an unmarked police car, with only a single blue light on the roof to signify it was anything other than ordinary. The fact that there were no seatbelts in the car did not bother us, until the driver burst on to the autostrada in the fast lane and we hurtled along at around 140 kph, often approaching the car in front with only a foot to spare before it moved into the middle lane to let us through. I had not experienced anything like that before and it was real white-knuckle stuff.

As the Italian countryside flashed past us, our thoughts were on what had been happening in the ten months since the discovery of Meredith in her cottage. The facts of the investigation had been relayed to us by our lawyer, and as we hurtled along the autostrada I tried to make some sense of them, wondering how many new details we would learn at the pretrial.

Immediately on discovering Meredith's body, top forensic scientists from Rome – headed by Patrizia Stefanoni, who had an international reputation as a forensic special-ist, and who had worked on identifying victims of the Far Eastern tsunami – had been introduced to the crime scene to collect DNA and other evidence. This was important, as these people were highly respected in Europe in the field of forensic science.

They had arrived at the crime scene wearing their white protective suits and gloves to avoid any contamination of the evidence they might find. DNA evidence, we were to learn, was to play a crucial part in the prosecution's case against Amanda Knox, Raffaele Sollecito and Rudy Guede. Patrizia Stefanoni was later to testify that the DNA of Amanda Knox was found on the handle of a kitchen knife, and Meredith's DNA was on the tip of the knife that was found by police in Sollecito's apartment. She said that when the knife was discovered, there were strange diagonal scrapes on the knife, which were consist-ent with the knife having been 'vigorously cleaned'.

Vital pieces of evidence for the prosecution also came from the footprints that were found in the cottage. Knox's prints had been found in the hallway and in Filomena Romanelli's room. Sollecito's had also been found in the bathroom.

The chemical luminol was used by the forensic police to expose these footprints. It is usually used by foren-sic crime investigators to determine blood that cannot be seen by the naked eye, because someone has attempted to clean it up. Small particles of blood, I learned, can cling to surfaces for many years without being seen.

Luminol is an important part of a forensic investigator's arsenal. When mixed with an appropriate oxidising agent at a crime scene, it reacts with the microscopic particles of iron in the blood, revealing microscopic traces of blood even if 'a partial but incomplete attempt has been made to clean the bloodstain away'. The area being investigated by forensic investigators is darkened, so that when luminol is used, the blood traces glow a bright blue for sufficient time to enable forensics to measure and photograph the print.

I learned that if bloodstains show up under luminol, but not to the naked eye, it is a near certainty that a crime scene clean-up has been attempted.

At the main trial in 2009, when Lorenzo Rinaldi, the director of the print identity division of the scientific police, was called to testify, he said, using visual demonstration on a screen in the court: 'From our investigations, we were able to conclude that the footprint found on the bath mat was compatible with that of Sollecito, as was one we found in the corridor outside, again using luminol. We also found that a naked footprint found in Knox's bedroom and in the corridor outside, again using luminol, was compatible with one taken from that person.'

The forensic specialists for the prosecution indicated that of those bloodied footprints attributed to Knox, one was shown exiting from her own bedroom and one was outside Meredith's room, facing into the room. More importantly, one footprint found in the room of

Meredith's Italian housemate, Filomena Romanelli, where the prosecution claimed that the break-in was staged, also contained the mixed DNA of Knox and Meredith. The forensic police said that Meredith's blood had been cleaned up in Romanelli's room, but was revealed using luminol.

On that mid-September day, as our police car drove into Perugia up the long, winding roads and steep hairpin bends, we were again reminded of the beauty of this part of the world. It was strange returning here, because already we felt a familiarity with the city. Our hotel was different from the one we had stayed in last time; it was a modern building a few minutes from the centre of the city, and had a secluded feel.

Before an hour has passed, our lawyer arrived at the hotel to brief us on what would be happening the following day. The proceedings for the pretrial, we were told, would be behind closed doors and no members of the press were allowed to be present. The appointed judge, Paolo Micheli, would have to determine from the evidence presented to him by both the chief prosecutor, Giuliano Mignini, and the defence lawyers for Amanda Knox, Raffaele Sollecito and Rudy Guede, whether or not they should stand trial for their alleged crimes.

Meanwhile, various legal wrangles had been evolving. Rudy Guede and his defence team were beginning to worry that the other defence teams might be attempting to pin the blame solely on him. Guede had written from his cell in the Capanne prison: 'It's simple for them to point the finger at me rather than themselves. Too many lies have been said about me by those who don't want the truth to surface.'

Guede's lawyer, Walter Biscotti, seemed to be as concerned as his client. 'There is a clear desire to make Rudy the guilty party,' he was quoted as saying, 'and it is clear that they will try anything.' He went on to add that 'there was a tacit agreement to just work on the defence of your own client, but it looks like this is finished.'

It was on the basis of these suspicions that Guede's defence requested that he be tried in full during the course of the pretrial. This is permissible under Italian law and is known as a 'fast-track trial'. If the request was granted, Guede would have the right to a select number of witnesses, but his case would not be heard by a jury of his peers, his fate instead decided by a single presiding judge. Anybody found guilty in a fast-track trial can look forward to a shorter sentence than they might have received in a full trial, since the reduction in the amount of time spent on the trial means it is less costly to the state, and so they incentivise with shorter sentences.

After considering the request, Judge Micheli granted Guede the fast-track trial. At the same time as deciding whether or not Knox and Sollecito would stand trial for Meredith's murder, he would have the responsibility of determining Guede's innocence or guilt, and then making the final decision as to his fate. Guede could be released or given a jail sentence, and Walter Biscotti declared that there would be no 'plea-bargaining'.

On Tuesday 16 September, just before 10 a.m., Stephanie, Arline and I arrived at the court. A discreet stone building at one end of a piazza, its entrance was swarming with reporters and press photographers. We had arrived in a police car and were glad of our escort as they guided us through the pack and into the quiet of the building itself. The thick stone walls and heavy wooden doors gave it a forbidding atmosphere and we all felt on edge as we were led to the courtroom.

Our seats were at the back and it was a strange sensation, to be sitting there, with a window to one side giving beautiful views of the countryside, while we waited for the accused and their lawyers to come in and take up their places.

We were accompanied by a translator, and Stephanie had a notebook in front of her to record anything that might be important. It was a nerve-wracking moment, but the most nerve-wracking of all was the moment when the door to the courtroom opened and Amanda Knox was led in by armed guards in berets and blue shirts. She looked nervously around her, and I kept looking at her. This was the first time that I had properly seen her, other than in newspaper photographs and on television news footage. The sight of guns in the holsters of the police and their grim expressions brought home to me the enormity of the moment. She was taken to a seat just four feet in front of us, and sat looking away so that we could not see her face. I kept staring at her, only catching glimpses of her when she half turned to talk to her lawyers. The police stationed themselves immediately behind and to the side of her.

Soon after Knox was seated, the door to the courtroom opened again and Rudy Guede was brought in, also under armed guard. I had expected a heavily built man, never having seen him before, other than head-and-shoulder shots in the press, but in the flesh he appeared to be quite slightly built. He sat some distance from us, next to his lawyer, and for the entire time that we were in court he remained completely expressionless, not even communicating with his lawyer. It was as if he was in a dream-like state.

Rafaello Sollecito was not present, his lawyer having said that he wanted to avoid the media circus that was surrounding the trial. Though this did not seem to be a problem for the court, I was surprised that they did not demand his presence. To me, it seemed to be a weak excuse for not attending.

As the hearing progressed, in a rush of Italian I could not understand, I struggled to concentrate on the snatches of information our translator passed to us. Instead, I was thinking about Meredith, and how I was only feet away from the people who were being charged with her murder. Only an arm's length away from me, Amanda Knox would occasionally smile at her defence team, but it was a smile that seemed to demand some form of reassurance rather than a return of pleasantries. No matter how hard I tried to make sense of the proceedings, I was constantly being drawn to look at her, catching her profile every time she made a small half-turn to her team.

Was this the woman, I kept thinking, who had taken my daughter's life away?

The day was gruelling, taken up with legal technicalities and documentation being passed between the various legal representatives. They had laptops open and were listening intently to the proceedings, but there was little to impart to us in the way of translation. On one occasion, our lawyer pointed out to us that when Amanda Knox had falsely accused Diya 'Patrick' Lumumba of being Meredith's killer, she was not, at that point, a suspect, but was simply helping with information. The prosecutor, Giuliano Mignini, made a point of saying that the idea that Knox had implicated Lumumba whilst under stress was inaccurate. He illustrated how, while Meredith's friends were upset by the killing, Knox had not shown any stress.

'They all showed a willingness to help,' he said, 'to establish the truth. Amanda Knox had no reason to feel fearful and stressed, unless she was involved in the crisis.'

At one point, we adjourned to a smoking room, where members of the police and lawyers could enjoy a cigarette. Mr Mignini was smoking a pipe. I pointed to it, not having seen anyone smoking a pipe for some years, and he smiled and genially offered it to me. I declined, because I have never been drawn to pipe smoking. At that moment, though, I wished that I did have a comforting habit to turn to: I felt stretched thin by tension, and I knew Arline and Stephanie did too.

In the evening, slightly bewildered and confused as to what had actually been said in court because it was couched in legal technicalities, we were asked to attend a press conference at our hotel. Despite the fact that it was difficult for us to present anything new, since there had not been any developments, we agreed. Stephanie prepared a statement, which she read to the press in both English and Italian:

'It is so easy to understand why Meredith loved this city. She loved everything about Italy, but the fact that she chose Perugia above all others showed that it was a special place for her. Perugia is definitely a place of culture, a beautiful place to meet people and learn. We only wish that Meredith had had more time before being brutally taken from us.

'Meredith was such a genuine person that when you think of her now and see her friends, you don't need to say anything; you only need to smile. We are all struggling to understand why she was so cruelly taken from us, but we are pleased that we have reached a new stage in the process, hoping that justice will soon be done for Meredith.'

That evening, we had dinner in the hotel restaurant with our lawyer, where the staff were marvellously sensitive and kind. We did not want to go into town in case we were followed by the press. Then, the next morning, we left Perugia to return to England, still numb, still shell-shocked, still unable to find the words to express – even amongst ourselves – what we were feeling.

In our absence, the fast-track trial of Rudy Guede continued concurrently with the judge's deliberations as to whether Knox and Sollecito would stand trial.

As was Guede's right, two witnesses testifying to his character appeared, but the real drama was in what was described as a 'super-witness' for the prosecution. An Albanian taxi driver, Hekuran Kokomani, aged thirty-four, had emerged from the shadows after several months to claim that he had been 'threatened' by Amanda Knox on either the night of the murder or the night before it. He claimed that he had not gone to the police earlier because he was scared, but that eventually he had been persuaded by a lawyer to do so.

In his testimony, Kokomani claimed to have been driving his VW Golf on the Via della Pergola near the cottage where Meredith lived but stopped on noticing what appeared to be bin bags in the road, whereupon Amanda Knox and Raffaele Sollecito emerged from the darkness.

'The girl had a black scarf around her neck,' he told the court, 'which partially covered her face. She started screaming at me, and pulled a knife out of a bag. It was about eight inches long. She was screaming at me: "Come on then!" The boy had a similar knife. Something in their eyes troubled me. They looked off their heads.'

He later changed his testimony to say that he had not been directly threatened with the knife, adding that Rudy Guede had also emerged, claiming that the knife Amanda was holding had been used to cut a cake in the cottage. Guede, he testified, had asked to borrow his car, which Kokomani refused. Kokomani claimed that he had recognised Guede at the time because he had met him before, but that it was only when the story of Meredith's murder had appeared in the newspapers that he had recognised Knox and Sollecito.

Kokomani's testimony was troubling, and made me picture more vividly what had happened on the night of Meredith's murder – but this was not the only troubling statement he was to make. 'Later,' he claimed, 'I heard that people were looking for me to offer me up to 100,000 euros not to speak to the police. I was scared.'

The defence lawyers attempted to say that his testimony was unreliable and, eventually, he was disregarded as being an unreliable witness. However, this was not the last time Kokomani would appear in court; he would be called upon again, when Knox and Sollecito faced their own trials.

Some people questioned whether he was telling the truth. Yet back in England, trying to keep track of everything that was happening, I could not help wondering what his motivation might have been if he truly was concocting this story. It is true that, in some cases, certain people put themselves forward as witnesses just to grab the limelight for themselves. However, it seemed perfectly reasonable to me that, after the murder, he was scared. If he had wanted to attract attention to himself, he would have approached the police earlier, when the full focus of attention would have been on him. The only thing that seemed questionable to me was that he could not remember whether it was the night of Halloween, 31 October, or 1 November, the night of the murder, that he saw the trio at the cottage. Also, he was said to have claimed that it was raining on the night in question, when it was shown not to have been.

As Guede's fast-track trial proceeded, Judge Micheli was also hearing evidence pertaining to Amanda Knox and Raffaele Sollecito, to determine whether they would face a trial by jury. As well as listening carefully through several sessions, he had been presented with 10,000 pages of documentation by the prosecution that outlined the evidence. He also heard evidence from forensics experts regarding the various DNA findings, Sollecito's DNA having been discovered on Meredith's bra clasp, and a bloodied footprint having been revealed as belonging to the young Italian man. On top of this, there was the presentation of evidence that Knox's bloodied footprints had been found in the hallway of the cottage and in the bathroom; that her DNA had been found in blood mixed with Meredith's in the bathroom; and that her DNA had been shown to be on a knife handle, with Meredith's on the blade, a knife that police had found at Sollecito's apartment and which, the prosecution claimed, had been removed from the scene of the crime.

Judge Micheli had also heard Knox's and Sollecito's defence teams attempting to refute much of the evidence, specifically the DNA evidence, which they blamed on contamination and poor forensics procedures. This was to be a major contention in this pretrial, the main trial and, later, the first appeal.

Regrettably, a key piece of evidence – Meredith's bra clasp – was not retrieved from the crime scene for forensic testing until 47 days after the murder, because it had been hidden from view and officers hadn't seen it.

Regarding her client's DNA being found on Meredith's bra clasp, one of Sollecito's lawyers, Giulia Bongiorno, argued: 'This is not a genetic tracer belonging to one single person, but a mix, resulting from contamination, and, therefore, should not be admitted as evidence in court.' A mannequin was brought into the courtroom and a demonstration given with a bra to try to show how contamination could have taken place.

The assistant prosecutor, Manuela Comodi, riposted by returning with a white bra to show how contamination could not have taken place.

The verbal battles continued, with Eduardo Giobbi, a detective with Rome's Serious Crime Squad, claiming: 'All three left traces of their presence at the scene of the crime, and were involved. We are convinced of that.'

And Chief of Police Arturo de Felice said: 'All three participated in this crime. The motive was sexual and the victim rebelled. Meredith was morally innocent.'

*   *   *

Based on all the evidence that emerged during Guede's fast-track trial, and the evidence presented by the prosecution, Judge Micheli now had to decide whether Rudy Guede was guilty of being involved in Meredith's murder, and whether there was sufficient evidence to send Knox and Sollecito for trial. It was to be a long deliberation.

Back in England, we knew that as soon as the judge was ready to make his decision, we would be returning to Perugia. All we could do was debate the evidence amongst ourselves, because we had no idea what the outcome would be. Between ourselves, we were almost convinced that, on the basis of the evidence that the prosecution had presented, Knox and Sollecito would have to be sent for trial. Yet we still had a niggling doubt as to whether or not this would take place. And if Knox and Sollecito did not have to face a trial, who, then, was responsible for Meredith's murder? We were already positive that Guede alone could not have overpowered her so easily. If the judge was to decide that the evidence against Knox and Sollecito did not demand a trial, the question would remain: who else killed my daughter?

On 28 October 2008, Arline, Stephanie, Lyle and I returned to Perugia to hear Judge Micheli's verdict. It was a nerve-wracking moment for us. Early that afternoon, we sat in our hotel reception area with our lawyer, Mr Maresca, a representative from the British Consulate in Florence and an interpreter from Rome, awaiting a call as to when we should travel to the court for the verdict. No one present knew what to expect. At first, we were given to understand that we would be on our way mid-afternoon. Yet time dragged on, and still no call came. We thought that it might be six o'clock, then eight. Eventually, we were told to be at the court for 9 p.m., and the police drove us there.

A crowd of press photographers jostled at the entrance, and we had to be guided in individually by police escorts. I felt almost light-headed with lack of sleep; looking at Arline, Stephanie and Lyle, I saw the same strain on their faces. Sitting at the rear of the courtroom with our interpreter, there was a tense silence. Amanda Knox sat with her lawyers, as did Raffaele Sollecito and Rudy Guede with theirs. They had all been led in individually under armed guard. This was the first time that we had seen Raffaele Sollecito and so my attention was focused on him. I could see why the media had referred to him as a Harry Potter lookalike. He seemed quite reserved. There did not, strangely enough, appear to be any glimmer of nervousness on his face. If anything, he appeared quite bewildered as to why he was there. Then, at last, I saw him move, and there was a flicker of a nervous smile. He did not look around the court, but simply sat down with his lawyers. Guede, meanwhile, was as expressionless as he had been before, not even talking to his lawyer. I found this lack of emotion particularly distressing, as it was Guede who would know his certain fate in only a few short minutes.

After a painful wait, Judge Micheli entered. Complete silence ensued as everyone rose to their feet. The chief of

Homicide, Monica Napoleone, stood at my side, ready to convey the verdict. As the judge began his statement, Ms Napoleone looked at me several times, squeezing my hand, then concentrating intensely on what the judge was saying.

Everything was in Italian, so we had no idea what was being said. I looked at the suspects to see if there was any indication from their expressions, but there was nothing.

The judge had been deliberating for twelve hours about his decision. This was the moment.

Monica Napoleone suddenly turned to look at me and squeezed my hand again, nodding emphatically. We then learnt that Rudy Guede had been found guilty of complicity in Meredith's murder and sentenced to thirty years in prison, and that Knox and Sollecito had been indicted on charges of murder and sexual violence and would stand trial.

Because Ms Napoleone had only a limited knowledge of English, the full impact did not hit us until our interpreter explained to us what had happened. I did not know what to feel, or what I ought to have been feeling. I can only say that we were not elated – but we were, at least, satisfied that justice was progressing in the right direction.

It is difficult to say what you feel at a time like this. It was certainly not relief, because I knew that this was, in effect, only the beginning. After this, we would have to go through the main trial. One day, we would be standing in the same spot, waiting to hear the verdicts on Knox and Sollecito, and it was not a moment any of us could relish.

When we left the court through a rear entrance, it was frightening. We had been told that up to 200 photographers were waiting outside. Each with our own police escort, we attempted to walk through the 'corridor' between the members of the press, who were scrambling for pictures. The police stood with their arms linked, trying to hold back the photographers, but they still surged forwards, under an explosion of flashbulbs. I had never before been at the heart of such a baying mob, and could not have predicted how terrifying the experience would be. Convinced that I was going to be knocked to the ground and trampled, I found myself propelled by my police escort until we reached the relative safety of the police vehicles. Once we were inside, the press flattened themselves against the windows. The car began to rock back and forth under their weight before it could finally edge out of the small compound into the street.

We were once more asked to do a press conference, which at this time of the evening was tiring. Yet, drained by the day's events, we agreed. Sitting at a long desk facing another barrage of cameras and film crews, we were asked if we were 'pleased' with the verdict. Lyle replied that 'pleased' was not really the word, more 'satisfied'.

We had dinner with our lawyer, but there was little for us to discuss. Guede had been sentenced and there was still a long way to go before we would know the verdicts on Knox and Sollecito. We would, we were told, be waiting at least a year before that day would come. Around our dinner table, we raised our glasses to Meredith and, privately, held on to memories of her. It was all that we could do.

In the meantime, Judge Micheli was obliged under Italian law to present a report as to how he had reached his decisions in both the pretrial and Guede's fast-track trial. I was to find this report invaluable, as it is not something I could have expected from either the British or the American legal systems.

The judge's 101-page report was published ninety days later, and his reasoning was damning against not only Guede, but Knox and Sollecito as well.

At the beginning of his sentence report on the conviction of Rudy Guede, as translated on the True Justice website, Judge Micheli stated that it was neither the place nor his intention to make the case against either Raffaele Sollecito or Amanda Knox. However, according to the nuances of the case, it was impossible not to involve them at all, for they were intimately involved with the events of the morning when Meredith's body was discovered.

Micheli dedicated quite a few pages of his report to the exact locations, positions, descriptions and measurements of all the items and bloodstains found in Meredith's room when the investigators arrived. He also went into precise details on the injuries, marks, cuts and bruises that were found when Meredith's body was examined in situ at the cottage, before she was moved. Despite their extent, it was obvious that these details were only a summary of the initial police report, which related in even more detail the extent of the ordeal to which she had been subjected.

It was these details that allowed the prosecution to lay out their scenario for the events, which they said must have happened in the room. It was also these details that convinced Micheli that it was impossible for this crime to have been carried out by a single person. In his report, he dismissed completely the scenarios presented by the defences of Knox and Sollecito for a 'lone wolf killing'. Micheli said that he was convinced that Meredith was sexually assaulted and then murdered by multiple attackers.

As well as outlining the reasons he found Guede guilty of murder, Micheli also addressed his reasons for deciding that Knox and Sollecito should stand trial. He noted Raffaele's apparent lies about the time he made the 112 (emergency services) phone calls. He dismissed Sollecito's defence's claim that the disposal of Meredith's phones did not allow time for Sollecito to get to the cottage after watching his film, kill Meredith and then dispose of the phones in Via Sperandio. He noted that Meredith's cell phone had logged a brief 10.13 p.m. call to the bank and had also picked up Meredith's calls home.

Micheli also noted that the police found both Knox's and Sollecito's behaviour suspicious almost straight away. He noted that Filomena Romanelli had said that the relationship between Amanda Knox and Meredith had deteriorated by October. This was something that we knew of from her friends in Perugia, and also from what Meredith had told us.

Micheli also refuted the claim that cannabis may have caused any loss of Knox's or Sollecito's memories.

Judge Micheli said that he based his decision on the following points of evidence.

1. After hearing both prosecution and defence arguments about Meredith's and Amanda's DNA on the knife and Raffaele's DNA on Meredith's bra clasp, the judge accepted the prosecution argument that both were valid evidence. He did note, however, that he fully expected that the same argument would be heard again at the full trial.

2. Judge Micheli explained that blood evidence proved that Meredith was wearing her bra when she was killed. Nor was it only the blood on her bra that demonstrated this. It was also where the blood *wasn't* on her body. Micheli said that Meredith was wearing her bra normally when she lay in the position in which she died. Her bra strap marks and the position of her shoulder were imprinted in the pool of blood in that position. Meredith's shoulder also showed signs that she lay in that position for quite some time.

Micheli then asked the question: Who came back to the room, cut off Meredith's bra and moved her body sometime later? It was not Rudy Guede. He went home, cleaned himself up and went out on the town with his friends. Judge Micheli reasoned in his report that it could only have been done by someone who knew about Meredith's death and had an interest in arranging the scene in Meredith's room. Seemingly, who else but Amanda Knox?

Knox was apparently the only person in Perugia that night who could gain access to the cottage. And the clasp that was cut with a knife when Meredith's bra was removed was found on 2 November 2007, when Meredith's body was moved by investigators. It was right under the pillow that had been placed under Meredith when she was moved by someone from the position in which she had died. On that clasp and its inch of fabric was the DNA of Raffaele Sollecito.

Micheli reasoned in his report that Raffaele and Amanda seemed to have returned to the cottage sometime after Meredith was dead, cut off her bra, moved her body, and staged the scene in Meredith's room.

3. Micheli explained that the claim that Rudy entered the cottage through the window in Romanelli's room was a very unlikely scenario, and that the evidence also indicated otherwise. He also said that the height and position of the window would expose any climber to the full glare of traffic headlights from cars on Via della Pergola. He asked, Why wouldn't a thief choose to break in through a ground-floor window of the empty house?

He further stated that the broken glass and marks on the shutter both demonstrated that the window was broken from the inside, some of the glass even falling on top of Filomena Romanelli's clothes, which had been thrown around the room to simulate a robbery.

But his major reason for believing that Rudy entered through the front door was the bloody footprints that showed up with luminol and fitted Knox's and Sollecito's feet. These suggested that the two of them had entered Filomena's room and created the scene in there after Meredith was killed.

Micheli reasoned that the only person who could have witnessed Rudy Guede's earlier sex assault on Meredith, who could gain entry via the front door, and had an interest in altering the crime scene in the house, appeared to be Amanda Knox. In his report, Micheli stated that this logic led him to believe that Amanda Knox was the one who let Rudy Guede into the cottage through the front door.

4. He examined the evidence of the homeless person, Antonio Curatolo, who claimed to have seen Knox and Sollecito in the vicinity of the cottage several times on the night of the killing. He said that although Curatolo mixed up his dates in his statement, he did have a fix on the night that he saw Knox and Sollecito in Piazza Grimana, sometime around 11.00 to 11.30 p.m. Curatolo was certain that it was the night before the piazza filled up with policemen asking if anyone had seen Meredith. In his evidence, he said that they came into the square from the direction of Via Pinturicchio and kept looking towards the cottage on Via della Pergola, from a position in the square where they could see the entrance gate.

Micheli also reasoned in his report that their arrival in Via Pinturicchio tied in with evidence from one of

Meredith's neighbours, Nara Capezzali, an elderly widow who lived on Meredith's street. Capezzali testified that she heard someone run up the stairs in the direction of that street. He also reasoned that it was likely that they were watching the cottage to see if Meredith's scream had resulted in the arrival of the police or for other activity.

5. Examining the evidence of Hekuran Kokomani, he found him to be far from discredited. He said that the testimony was garbled and his dates and times made no sense, but that Kokomani was in the vicinity of the cottage on both 31 October and 1 November 2007 was not in doubt.

Furthermore, Micheli said that when Kokomani gave his statement, he described seeing a car that had broken down on Via della Pergola, and a tow truck that had come to its aid. Pasqualino Coletta, a tourist who was visiting Perugia in November 2007, had testified that his car had broken down on the night of 1 November (the night Meredith was killed). The same breakdown was also seen by a young woman who was walking down the street at the time, Alessandra Formica. The details Kokomani gave about the breakdown seemed to place him in the vicinity of the cottage Knox and Meredith shared on the night of the murder. Alessandra Formica also testified that a young black man, who she later identified as Guede, had violently bumped into her boyfriend at about 10.30 or 10.40 p.m. on the 1 November. He didn't stop or apologise, he just carried on running.

So Micheli argued that Kokomani was definitely near the cottage right around the time of Meredith's murder and he, in turn, placed Sollecito, Knox and Guede together outside the cottage at the same time. His evidence also placed all three outside the cottage at some time the previous night.

Judge Micheli found that all this evidence implicated Amanda Knox and Raffaele Sollecito as accomplices of Rudy Guede in the murder of Meredith.

By the time our family had returned to England to debate once again everything that had happened at the pretrial, former FBI employee Clint Van Zandt, talking to NBC News, gave an unbiased opinion: 'These are good cops,' he said. 'They are linking together all of the technology: cell phones, the Internet, the crime scene, forensic evidence. I think that, when this is all over and done with, we'll find out what happened to Meredith on that terrible night.'

We had no fault with the Italian justice system, despite protestations from some quarters in America that it was flawed. In fact, I was even heartened by the idea of reading such a detailed report explaining how Judge Micheli had come to his verdicts. Where else in the world, I wondered, would judges be required to write such lengthy reports on their decisions? Where else would any suspects, later found guilty, be awarded the right to two appeals, one to the court that convicted them and one to the Supreme Court? As the year progressed, and as the main trial got

under way, accusations would be flung from all directions, calling the justice system into doubt and seemingly
demanding Knox and Sollecito's release without any real
reasoning.

But, as a family, all of that was secondary to what we
were going through. In our hearts, all we wanted to know
was what had happened to Meredith and why she had to
be taken so cruelly away.

7

The Trial

The trial of Amanda Knox and Raffaele Sollecito began at the start of 2009, but, at first, we were not required to go to Perugia. Part of me wanted to be there and follow the trial in full, but we knew it would be a lengthy affair, and not one that we would be able to understand completely. All the same, we did know that, at some point, we would be required to return and provide our various testimonies concerning Meredith. So, too, would we have to listen to the evidence again, and relive the night of Meredith's death, which was distressing for us all. In the meantime, we would have to wait and follow the progress of the trial from afar. We learned of events via Francesco Maresca on a weekly and, sometimes, a daily basis. Throughout, it was frustrating, and it constantly felt as if we should have been doing more, but our hands were tied and we could not afford to stay in Perugia for several months.

The Foreign Office does not offer financial help to the families of victims of crime abroad, not even so that they can attend the trials of those accused of killing their loved ones. On reflection, we would not have wanted to have been in Perugia for the duration of the trial as it would have been too stressful, not only because of our inability to understand the language, but also because of work commitments and Arline being on dialysis three times a week. We felt that it was sufficient for us to visit Perugia when requested to do so at important parts of the trials.

The case that the prosecution put forward rested not only on the DNA evidence and the alleged staged break-in, but also on the conflicting alibis of Amanda Knox and Raffaele Sollecito, which had changed on several occasions.

The prosecutor, Mr Mignini, outlined that Raffaele Sollecito originally told police investigators that, on the afternoon of 1 November 2007, he and Knox had left the cottage on Via della Pergola at 6 p.m., and that they went for a walk to the town. They passed through Piazza Grimana, Piazza Morlacchi and by the main fountain in Corso Vannucci.

Amanda Knox, meanwhile, told investigators that this had happened an hour earlier, at 5 p.m., and that they had then gone straight to Sollecito's apartment.

According to Sollecito, he and Amanda were at a friend's party on the night of the murder – yet no alibis were ever found to prove that this was true. Afterwards, Sollecito initially claimed, he had spent all night at his apartment alongside Amanda, yet his DNA was found at the cottage on Meredith's bra clasp, alongside a bloodied footprint that forensic experts for the prosecution matched to his trainers. He said that he had downloaded and watched the film *Amélie* on his computer during the night. However, a computer expert, Mr Trotta, introduced by the prosecution, said that the film had actually been watched at around 6.30 p.m.

On 5 November, however, Sollecito told police that Knox had gone to meet friends at Patrick Lumumba's bar, Le Chic, at around 9 p.m., and that she did not return until about 1 a.m. He was recorded as saying to investigators: 'At 9 p.m. I went home alone, and Amanda said that she was going to Le Chic because she wanted to meet some friends. We said goodbye. I went home, rolled myself a spliff of marijuana, and made some dinner.' No witnesses were produced to say that Knox had been at the bar.

Sollecito claimed that he had spoken to his father at 11 p.m. But telephone records obtained by the police showed that there was no telephone conversation at this time. Sollecito's father had called him a couple of hours earlier, at 8.40 p.m.

Sollecito also claimed to police that he was alone, surfing the Internet from 11 p.m. to 1 a.m., but no technical evidence of this was introduced. Computer experts testified on behalf of the prosecution that his computer was not used for an eight-hour period on the night of Meredith's murder.

According to Amanda Knox's statements to the police, on the night of Meredith's murder she had not replied to

Patrick Lumumba's text message that she was not needed at the bar that evening. The police knew that this was not true, because they already had her mobile-phone records proving that she had, indeed, texted him.

Amanda said to police: 'After that [finding out that she was not required to work at Le Chic that night] I believe that we relaxed in his [Sollecito's] room together; perhaps I checked my emails.' However, police say that no Internet activity at all was proven at Sollecito's apartment beyond the early evening. 'One thing that I do remember,' Amanda went on to say, 'is that I took a shower with Raffaele, and this might explain how we passed the time. In truth, I do not remember exactly what day it was, but I do remember that we had a shower and that we washed ourselves for a long time. He cleaned my ears and he dried and combed my hair.'

Yet, according to the prosecution, Sollecito made no mention of having taken a shower with Amanda on the night of the murder.

They then went on to explain that, in Amanda's handwritten note to the police, she had claimed that she and Sollecito ate at around 11 p.m. 'One of the things that I am sure about,' she said, 'that definitely happened the night that Meredith was murdered, was that Raffaele and I ate fairly late. I think around 11 p.m.'

However, when the trial commenced, Knox testified that she and Sollecito ate at around 9.30 p.m. 'After we ate,' she said, 'Raffaele washed the dishes. But the pipes under his sink broke and water flooded the floor.'

Both Knox and Sollecito had claimed to police that they woke up late on the morning of 2 November. However, according to the prosecution's evidence, their mobile-phone records showed that both their mobiles were turned on at approximately 6.02 a.m. According to computer analysts for the prosecution, Sollecito also used his computer at 5.32 a.m.

The prosecution went on to claim that, at 12.08 p.m. on 2 November, the day after Meredith was murdered, Amanda Knox had called her Italian housemate Filomena Romanelli. In that conversation, Knox told Filomena that she had discovered the front door to their cottage open, and some bloodstains in the cottage's small bathroom.

Knox told police that she made this call from Sollecito's apartment. Yet, in his prison diary, Sollecito later described the same conversation as taking place while they were both at the cottage.

Knox claimed that she had then called Meredith's Italian phone, the one Romanelli had lent her, but that it 'just kept ringing and without any answer'. Yet both the police and the prosecution said Knox's mobile-phone records showed that this call lasted just three seconds, while the call to Meredith's British phone lasted only four seconds.

The prosecution outlined that, at 12.34 p.m. on the same day, Amanda and Filomena again spoke to each other on their phones. Filomena told police: 'We spoke to each other for the third time, and she told me that the window in my room was broken, and that my room was in a mess. At this point, I asked her to call the police, and she said that she already had.'

However, the prosecution introduced records to show that Knox and Sollecito did not actually call the police until 12.51 p.m.

The prosecution went on to show that, in an email to friends in Seattle on 4 November, Knox claimed that she had called Meredith's phones after speaking to Filomena. Yet police records showed that this was untrue. In the email in question, Amanda also claimed that she had called Filomena back forty-five minutes later, after Raffaele had finished calling the police at 12.55 p.m. Yet again, records showed that Knox had never called Filomena back at all.

The prosecution explained that Sollecito and Knox had both claimed they had called the police before the postal police had turned up at the cottage, and were waiting for them. Sollecito later said that this was not true, and that he had lied because he had believed Amanda Knox's version of what had happened.

Sollecito told police that he had gone outside the cottage 'to see if I could climb up to Meredith's window' but was unable to. 'I tried to force Meredith's bedroom door open, but couldn't and, at that point, I decided to call my sister for advice, because she is a *carabinieri* officer. She told me to dial 112 but, at that moment, the postal police arrived.'

He then added: 'In my former statement, I told you a load of rubbish, because I believed Amanda's version of what happened, and did not think about the inconsistencies.'

The prosecution said Knox's mobile-phone records showed that she had called her mother, Edda Mellas, in Seattle at 12.47 p.m. Edda Mellas claimed that she told Amanda to hang up and call the police. However, according to the prosecution, Amanda made no mention of this advice from her mother when describing their decision to call the police. Knox even testified that she could not remember telephoning her mother.

In London, I found the information all quite confusing. It seemed that as soon as the court was presented with one version of the events of 1 and 2 November, a new version would emerge, changing every time the alibis of the suspects did. Originally, for instance, Knox had said that she was with Sollecito throughout the evening; later, that she had been at the cottage in the kitchen, where she had heard Meredith scream and had covered her ears. In Perugia, the jury, consisting of six ordinary members of the public, would have to consider why there were so many conflicting alibis from both Knox and Sollecito. They would have to weigh up these various scenarios.

The prosecution went on to show that, as well as telling seemingly contradictory stories about the events of the morning after Meredith's murder, other facets of Amanda's statements to the police indicated a deliberate attempt at deception. Knox told police that she had seen Patrick Lumumba, whom she had falsely accused of killing Meredith, at the basketball court on the night of the murder, and that he was later in Meredith's bedroom with her. Witnesses for Lumumba, however, testified that at that time he was at his bar, Le Chic.

Amanda also claimed that she had been 'hit' by police at the police station when being questioned, but even her own defence lawyers had stated during the pretrial that they had never said that, only that she was 'put under pressure'.

In her statements, Amanda had repeatedly claimed that 'Meredith was my friend'. Upon hearing this, my family and I were naturally upset. Meredith had constantly complained to her friends and our family that she was unnerved about the strange men Amanda brought home, and also about Amanda's bad hygiene habits. A friend of Meredith's also stated that on a return flight to London from Perugia, Meredith had complained about Amanda for almost the entire journey.

The jury was going to have to weigh up all of these complex inconsistencies to try to determine a logical sequence of events. Meanwhile, back in England, my family and I were trying to do exactly the same. Yet for every answer the trial seemed to provide, a dozen new questions raised their heads – and, the longer things went on, the more difficult it was, trying to piece together the things that had been said. Would Meredith, we wondered, not have told her potential killer that there was someone else in the house, if that was truly the case? Would a killer have dared to perpetrate his act while Amanda Knox was in the kitchen 'covering her ears', as she later stated? If this was really the case, why had Amanda not rushed to Meredith's aid, especially if – as she claimed – they were in fact good friends? Why did she not telephone the police? Why did neither she nor Rudy Guede telephone the emergency services to save Meredith's life? Why, if Rudy was, as he said, in the toilet, did Amanda never mention that he was in the house? Rudy was, after all, the only one of the three to have admitted to being in the cottage on the night of the killing. And why were the alibis she later used to explain her whereabouts on that terrible evening so inconsistent?

Meanwhile, we found it increasingly difficult to accept the suggestion that Meredith had had consensual sex on the night of her murder. The Meredith we knew was not the sort of girl who would have gone with a stranger, and the idea that she had simply let Rudy Guede into the cottage and her bedroom without any protest seemed ridiculous to us all.

At the end of March 2009, an important witness for the prosecution took the stand. He was a vagrant named Antonio Curatolo, who had frequented the various areas of Perugia for almost a decade. With his long white beard and hair, he looked unkempt, but we were told that, on the stand, he was articulate and appeared to be convinced of what he had seen on the night of Meredith's murder.

From the stand, Curatolo told the court that he spent a lot of his time hanging around Corso Garibaldi, where Sollecito lived, and also around Piazza Grimani. Between

9.30 and 10 p.m. on the night of Meredith's murder, he was in Piazza Grimani itself, and observed two people sitting next to one another. He was asked by the court to describe them, and he looked across at where Amanda was sitting with her lawyers. 'It was her . . .' he said. He then looked at Sollecito, sitting quietly and looking detached, and added, '. . . and him.' Curatolo said that he had seen them separately before, but that evening was the first time he had seen them together. He told the court that he was not particularly watching them all of the time, but that he did see them again at around midnight in the same location.

The jury obviously had to consider his story because, if his testimony was correct, then it would contradict Sollecito's and Knox's alibis that they spent the evening at Sollecito's place – although, of course, it must be remembered that Sollecito did change his story to say that Amanda had left his place at 9 p.m. and returned at 1 a.m.

Curatolo said it was at midnight that he left the piazza for the park to get some sleep. He returned to the piazza the next day, 2 November, at around 12.00 p.m. and at 1.30 p.m. saw the *carabinieri* pass, and also more police and crime-scene people.

Sollecito's defence lawyer, Giulia Bongiorno, asked Curatolo how he could possibly have known that it was 9.30 p.m. on the night of 1 November, but he was completely unshaken by the question. He replied: 'Because the sign next to the piazza has a digital clock. I also have a watch, and I look at it often to check the time. When I sat on the bench to read, I looked at my watch, and it was just before 9.30 p.m., and I saw them shortly afterwards.'

Another witness for the prosecution was able to draw definite connections between Knox, Sollecito and Guede. Fabrizio Giofreddi testified that on 30 October 2007, he had parked his car at the junction where Via della Pergola, on which Meredith's cottage was situated, leads up to Piazza Grimani. Asked if he was certain of the date, he replied that he was, because when he was leaving he scratched the car next to him and left a note for the driver of the other car, writing down the necessary information, including the date and time.

He said that when he had arrived and parked his car, at about 5 p.m., he saw four people walking from the driveway of the cottage on to the road. Giofreddi alleged that he saw Amanda, Raffaele, Meredith and a black man he was ninety-nine per cent certain was Rudy Guede, because he had seen him before. In addition, he said that he had seen them all so clearly that he could even tell the court what they had been wearing.

He claimed that Meredith was wearing jeans, a dark coat and high heels; that Amanda had on a red coat with large buttons and jeans, and that Raffaele had on a long, dark jacket and trousers. He said that, after noticing them, he had locked his car and gone on with his business. In the courtroom, he formally identified Knox and Sollecito as two of the people he had seen together that day.

When cross-examined by the defence as to why it had taken him a year to come forward with this information, he told the court that he had not seen its relevance until he had spoken with one of his teachers, who had persuaded him to go to the police.

In Italian courts, suspects are permitted to interject in the proceedings, and at this moment Raffaele Sollecito took advantage of this. Standing up, he declared, 'This witness could not have seen me with Rudy Guede because, as I have said, I do not know Rudy Guede, and I have never met him before in my life. Also, the day that he claims to have seen us all together is impossible, as I was somewhere else and that will be proved as the trial continues.'

Back in England, hearing this testimony was diffi-cult and confusing, for Giofreddi seemed to imply that Meredith had known and been on familiar terms with all three of the people implicated in her murder. I wondered why Giofreddi had waited so long to come forward with this testimony and if he might have been mistaken with the dates – but, more than that, I had to question his claim that Meredith was in the company of Rudy Guede. Meredith's friends in Perugia have always maintained that they had never seen Meredith with Guede on any occasion. I wondered if, perhaps, Meredith was going out for the evening and had left the cottage at the same time as Knox and Sollecito, purely coincidentally. As far as I could tell, the only reason that Guede could ever have been seen with Meredith was that he might have called at the cottage to meet Knox and Sollecito, just at the time Meredith was leaving. I did, however, find it particularly strange that Giofreddi could remember every item of clothing the quartet were wearing, a year after the event. My own memory does not work as strongly as that.

The court also heard from an elderly widow, Nara Capezzali, who took the stand as a witness for the prosecution. Her testimony was to send a shiver through those present in the courtroom, and is still unnerving to read. Mrs Capezzali, we learned, was one of Meredith's neighbours, living with her daughter in an apartment across from the cottage. Having taken the stand, she stated that she had gone to bed reasonably early on the night of 1 November, but had woken somewhere between 11.00 and 11.30 p.m. to go to her bathroom. It was at this point, she said, that she heard a terrifying and prolonged scream.

Questioned by the prosecutor, Giuliano Mignini, about the events of that night, her testimony makes deeply troubling reading. What follows is the testimony Mrs Capezzali provided as translated into English by the independent lawyers running the True Justice for Meredith Kercher website:

> Mrs Capezzali: 'I heard a scream; an agonising scream that made my skin creep. It was the voice of a woman. There was no cry for help. It was just a scream, then nothing. The scream left me really disturbed; even now it troubles me.'

Mr Mignini: 'Are you capable of knowing where the scream came from?'

Mrs Capezzali: 'Yes, from the cottage.'

Mr Mignini: 'From the house of Via della Pergola 7?'

Mrs Capezzali: 'Yes . . . I stayed watching through the window. I heard the trampling of gravel, of leaves, that came from the driveway. Then I heard running.'

Mr Mignini: 'How long after the scream?'

Mrs Capezzali: 'It could have been a few seconds; a minute.' Asked if she was looking through her window with her head outside, she replied: 'No, because I have plants, but I could see through the windowpane, which doesn't have shutters, only glass. Then I could hear running on the iron stairway.'

Mr Mignini: 'The iron stairway, where does it lead to?'

Mrs Capezzali: 'It goes from the car park and ends up at the Via del Melo, where there is an iron gate. And, shortly afterwards, to Via Pinturicchio.'

Mr Mignini: 'Someone was climbing these stairs, the iron stairway?'

Mrs Capezzali: 'Running.'

Mr Mignini: 'Running. A single person or more than one?'

Mrs Capezzali: 'At that point, I heard a single person.'

Mr Mignini: 'And someone else. But was there
someone else?'
Mrs Capezzali: 'Someone ran away from the driveway towards Via del Bulagaio.'

Back in London, I was intrigued by the testimonics
evolving in the courtroom. There seemed to be so many
witnesses to the events of that fateful night. Arline and I
spoke frequently on the telephone to discuss these events,
but we were still confused. Stephanie could understand
a little more than we could, because of her knowledge
of Italian, and she kept abreast of reports that were
published in the Italian newspaper *La Repubblica*, which
was closely following the case.

Further evidence came from Antonella Morlacchia,
a young woman living with her parents in Via
Pinturicchio, a street behind the parking facility. One
view from her apartment looks down over Via della
Pergola, where Meredith lived, allowing her to see the
cottage clearly. In court, she testified that on the night
of 1 November, she returned home between 11 and
11.30 p.m. and had gone to bed. Soon after, she was
awoken by the sound of people arguing; it sounded
to her like a man and a woman. She said that she had
looked out of her window but had not seen anyone.
However, the arguing was definitely coming from Via
della Pergola, although she was not certain whether it
was coming from the cottage.

Next on the stand was truck driver Giampaolo Lambrotti. On the evening of 1 November, Lambrotti had gone to the aid of a car that had broken down on the opposite side of the road from the cottage. On the stand, he testified that he had received the call to go to the car at around 10.30 to 10.40 p.m. and had arrived at approximately 11 p.m. From there, he claimed, he had a clear view of the cottage. When he arrived, he said that he had found two young men and two young women with the car. As he prepared their car for towing, he noticed that there was a small, dark-coloured car parked in front of the gate to 7 Via della Pergola, although he could not identify the make.

More important testimony came from Marco Quintavalle, a supermarket owner, who testified that he saw Amanda Knox standing outside his shop at around 7.45 a.m. on 2 November. He claimed that when he opened up the shop, she entered and went to the section where the cleaning products were kept. Though he testified that he was not certain what it was that she had bought, the police who made a search of Sollecito's home testified that they had found a receipt for cleaning products from the same shop. After the murder police found several bottles of bleach in Raffaelle's flat, but his cleaner confirmed that she had never seen bleach there before.

Quintavalle said that he had noticed the girl's 'incredible blue eyes', adding: 'I thought that it was very strange for a student to be out so early in the morning. That morning was virtually a holiday; there were no lectures.

If there had been, I could have understood her being up so early.' The girl, he said, walked off in the direction of the cottage where Meredith was killed. Asked if he recognised the girl in court, he indicated Amanda Knox.

A further indication of Knox's strange behaviour following the murder was provided by the owner of a local lingerie shop, Carlo Mario Scotto di Rinaldi, who told police that early on the evening of 3 November, only one day after the discovery of Meredith's body, and only the day after they had been questioned by police, Sollecito and Knox had visited his shop. He said that he could prove this, because they were recorded on the shop's CCTV cameras.

Mr Rinaldi, who said that he understood a reasonable amount of English, claimed: 'They were all over each other, all of the time, kissing and embracing. Their behaviour was so exhibitionist that the other customers were looking at them.' He said that Knox had bought a couple of thongs and a T-shirt. Then, when they came to pay for the items, he claimed that he overheard Sollecito saying to Knox: 'You can put these on at home and we can have wild sex.'

It was extremely disturbing for me to learn of this kind of incident, for it hardly showed that there was any sadness about Meredith's passing.

Despite police officers testifying under oath in court that Amanda Knox was well treated during the early days of her questioning immediately after Meredith's murder, she persistently stated that she was put under pressure by the police and that she was slapped on the back of the head. Curiously, one of her own defence lawyers, Luciano Ghirga, who was quoted as saying during the pretrial: 'There were pressures from the police, but we never said that she was hit.'

Police interpreter Anna Donnino told the court that Knox had been comforted by police at the police station and given food and drink, and that at no stage had she been hit or threatened. This was also confirmed by the head of Homicide, Monica Napoleone.

Other inconsistencies emerged when Amanda Knox took the stand and stated: 'I heard that there was a body in there [meaning Meredith's room]. There was lots of confusion. I was in shock. I couldn't believe what had happened, couldn't accept it.'

I remembered and noted that the important words were she 'heard that there was a body in there.' However, on 2 November, when Knox had gone to the police station, Meredith's friends said that 'she was almost proud to have found the body'. Police who intercepted Knox's emails to her friends before her arrest also said that she had claimed to have found Meredith's body. Yet when Luca Altieri, under Chief Inspector Battistelli's instructions, had broken down Meredith's door, it was noted that Knox and Sollecito were in a different room.

It was also noted by some of Meredith's friends, including Natalie Hayward, that Amanda Knox had said Meredith's body was by the wardrobe. In fact, when

Meredith was found, her body was on the floor covered by a duvet, away from the wardrobe. This strange inconsistency became even more troubling when Francesco Camona, a blood-pattern analyst, told the court, with photographic illustration: 'From the photographs of the blood pattern, we can see that when Meredith was fatally knifed in the throat, she was no more than 40 cm from the floor. She was kneeling down in front of the wardrobe, her face was pressed almost to the floor. She was on her knees with her chest pushed forwards and her legs behind her.'

Camona was suggesting that Meredith was killed in front of the wardrobe – exactly where Amanda Knox had incorrectly claimed she had found the body. Naturally, this set off a terrible chain of thought. How, I wondered, could Amanda Knox possibly have known the original position of Meredith's body if the body was actually discovered elsewhere, and if she was not even present when Meredith's bedroom door was kicked down?

When Amanda Knox was called to take the stand in the court, I was shocked to discover that her language was more like that of a high-school teenager than a mature young woman. She said of Meredith's death: 'It was a disgusting death. I imagined that it was a slow death; a death that was shocking, yucky, disgusting.' Upon hearing this, I could not forget the testimony of one of Meredith's friends who had said that when Amanda had arrived at the police station on the evening of 2 November, and they had asked the police if Meredith might have died in pain, Amanda had interjected: 'What do you think? She fucking bled to death.'

When Francesco Maresca stood up in court and enquired of Amanda whether she had suffered because of the death of her 'friend', Amanda Knox replied: 'Yes, I was very shocked. I remember Meredith, but in the end, I knew her for a month and, first of all, I'm trying to get on with my life.' This, I thought, was an extremely callous response regarding the murder of somebody with whom she was claiming to be friends.

Knox attempted to redress the balance by saying: 'I confided in Meredith. I would often ask her for advice. When Meredith had a problem over my behaviour, she would tell me. That was it. There was nothing that she would keep hidden or that we couldn't find agreement on.'

Yet this was not the impression I got when Meredith used to talk to me on the telephone and complain about Amanda's hygiene habits.

Later, Amanda's mother, Edda Mellas, took the stand. Regarding the relationship between Meredith and Amanda, she said: 'They got along great. She told me about the fun things that she and Meredith did.'

In fairness, there seemed no reason why Amanda might not have described her relationship with Meredith like this to her mother. However, this does sharply contrast with the fact that Meredith had told Arline that she had tried to include Amanda with her friends, but that Amanda had told her she did not want to consort with

English-speaking people as she preferred to immerse herself in the Italian language.

When Amanda testified, a major part of the questioning was conducted by the deputy prosecutor – known in Italy as the public minister – Ms Manuela Comodi. Ms Comodi's line of questioning concentrated on a telephone call that Amanda was said to have made to her mother on 2 November. This call, it was noted, was on Amanda's phone records. The questioning was conducted in English, and played out as follows:

Ms Comodi: 'You said that you called your mother on the morning of 2 November 2007.'

Amanda: 'Yes.'

Ms Comodi: 'When did you call her for the first time?'

Amanda: 'The first time was right away after they [the police] had sent us out of the house. I was like this. I called my mother.'

Ms Comodi: 'So this was when either the police or the *carabinieri* had already intervened?'

Amanda: 'It was after they had broken down the door and sent us outside. I don't know what kind of police it was, but the ones who arrived first. Later, many other people arrived.'

Ms Comodi: 'But from the records, we see that you called your mother at twelve. At midday. What time is it in Seattle, if in Perugia it is midday?'

Amanda: 'In Seattle, it's morning. It's a nine-hour difference, so three in the morning in Seattle.'

Ms Comodi: 'During the conversation that you had with her, in prison, even your mother was amazed that you her called her at midday, which was three or four o'clock in the morning in Seattle, to tell her that nothing had happened.'

Amanda: 'I didn't know what had happened. I just called my mother to say that [the police] had sent us out of the house and that I had heard something about . . .'

Ms Comodi: 'But at midday, nothing had happened yet, in the sense that the door had not been broken down yet.'

Amanda: 'Hm. OK, I don't remember that phone call. I remember that I called her to tell her something about a foot.' [This referred, I presume, to Meredith's foot having been visible from under the duvet when the door was broken down.]

Ms Comodi: 'But if you called her before, why did you do it?'

Amanda: 'I don't remember, but if I did, I would have called to . . .'

Ms Comodi: 'You did it.'

Amanda: 'OK, that's fine. But I don't remember it. I don't remember that phone call.'

At this stage, Judge Massei intervened with his own questions, in an attempt at clarification.

Judge Massei (to Amanda): 'Excuse me. You might

not remember it, but the public minister has just
pointed out to you a phone call that your mother
received in the small hours.'

Ms Comodi: 'At three o'clock in the morning.'

Judge Massei: 'So that must be true. That did
happen. Were you in the habit of calling her at
such an hour? Did you do this on other occasions? It's just that we don't usually call each
other in the middle of the night.'

Amanda: 'Yes, yes, that's true.'

Judge Massei: 'So either you had a particular reason
on that occasion, or else it was a routine. This is
what the public minister is referring to.'

Amanda: 'Yes. Well, since I don't remember this
phone call, although I do remember the one
that I made later. But obviously I made that
phone call. So, if I made that phone call, it's
because I had, or thought that I had, something
to tell her. Maybe I thought that, even then,
that there was something strange, because, at
that moment, when I'd gone to Raffaele's place,
I did think that there was something strange,
but I don't know what to think. But I really
don't remember that phone call, so I can't say,
for sure, why.'

Listening to this in England and reading transcripts,
I found it extremely confusing. It seemed as if Amanda
had no idea of what she was talking about. She could

not seem to remember an important telephone call to her mother concerning the events at the cottage.

Later, Knox's mother was questioned on the same topic, this time by a lawyer employed by Patrick Lumumba, who was in court because he was bringing an action for compensation from Knox for having wrongly accused him of killing Meredith.

Lawyer: 'Did you receive any calls from your daughter?'
Edda Mellas: 'Early morning on the second.'
Lawyer: 'How many?'
Edda Mellas: 'Three.'
Lawyer: 'What time in Seattle?'
Edda Mellas: 'The first around 4 a.m. Maybe some
   minutes before. The second call within an hour,
   and the third, shortly after the second. The first
   call, Amanda said: "I know it's early," but she
   called because she felt someone had been in her
   house. She had spent the night at Raffaele's. She
   came back to have a shower and the main door
   was open. She thought that it was odd, but it had
   a funny lock, and it did not close well. She went
   to have a shower, and when she came out, she
   noticed some blood, but she thought that maybe
   someone had had their menstrual cycle and did not
   clean it. She went to her room and then went to
   the other bathroom to dry her hair and saw that
   there were faeces in the bathroom. She thought
   that was strange, because girls normally flushed

the bathroom. She went back to Raffaele's and
told him about the things that she found strange.'

Edda Mellas also told the court that Amanda had tried
to call her other housemates and had got hold of one of
them sometime later. Mellas then testified that Amanda
had tried calling Meredith but had received no answer.
According to Mellas, Knox had then gone back to the
house with Raffaele and noticed the broken window in
Romanelli's room.

Yet the prosecution noticed some inconsistencies
in the testimony. They wondered, for instance, why
Amanda went home to have a shower, when she had
already said that, on the night of 1 November, she and
Raffaele had taken a shower together at his place. If
another shower was required, they asked, why did she
not use the shower at Sollecito's flat, where she claimed
to have woken up?

Furthermore, Edda Mellas had said that Amanda had
tried calling her housemates, one of whom she reached,
before she then tried to call Meredith to no avail, after
which she had gone back to the house. Yet, according
to Amanda Knox's testimony, it had been established
that she was already at the house when she had called
Filomena Romanelli and Meredith.

Raffaele Sollecito's father, Francesco, told the court: 'We
were always convinced as to the absolute innocence and
total strangeness of the allegations against Raffaele.' And

of Raffaele's relationship with Amanda, he said: 'He told me that he had just started a beautiful love story with Amanda. He loved and adored her. He spoke to me about her in a way that he had never done about other girls. Raffaele had a certain affection towards Amanda.'

Regarding the fact that Raffaele carried a knife in his pocket, his father said that this was something that he had done since he was a young boy living in the country. Commentators observed that doing this as a young boy was one thing, but carrying a knife, as an adult, in a university town such as Perugia, with residential areas, was quite another thing.

Our family received notification from Francesco Maresca that our presence would be required in court in the summer of 2009, to provide testimonies regarding Meredith. So, Stephanie, Arline, and I flew out to Perugia to fulfil this. Our lawyer told us that the entire family's presence was not necessary, and so John and Lyle remained in England. It was slightly unsettling for us, as this time, when we arrived at the airport, there was no police escort. We had to make our own way to the court, and none of us had ever been in a court before to take the stand under questioning. A handful of photographers were waiting to take our pictures, but we managed to secure a taxi to take us to our hotel. Having settled into our rooms, we were then able to get another taxi to the court, where the usual press contingent awaited us. We were met outside the court by one of the translators, who led us inside, where we had to wait in an austere area before being called into the court.

We had to be presented one by one into the court, so that we were unable to hear what one another was saying to the court. Two police officers standing outside with us commented on how Stephanie looked like Meredith's twin sister, a fact that many had commented on during their lives together.

Inside the court, we were provided with a translator, who translated the questions from our lawyer and the prosecutor into English for us, and then our answers into Italian, so that everyone in the court could understand.

Arline was the first one to be called to testify. When asked about Meredith, she said: 'Her death was unreal in many ways, and still is. I still look for her. We'll never, never get over this. It's such a shock to send your child to school and not have her come back.'

Stephanie took the stand to say: 'Meredith was really looking forward to coming to Perugia. She wanted to make the most of her year in Italy. She wanted to pick up the language and learn about the culture.' Although Stephanie could speak Italian, she spoke in English, as it was easier for her to do so and she felt more confident. Asked whether Meredith would have fought back against her attackers, she said: 'Absolutely. One hundred and ten per cent. Mez had a strong personality and, physically, she was very strong. She was very passionate about things that were important to her, family, friends and coming to Italy. She fought for her place here and she would have fought to the end.'

Once Arline and Stephanie had testified, it was time
for me to be called into the court. As they answered their
questions, I had been sitting outside, somewhat nervous. Despite being a journalist and having interviewed
thousands of people, I was suddenly quite self-conscious
about being questioned myself. Outside, it had been like
that classic scene in a comedy, where you are all sitting
together and then, one by one, the people next to you
disappear, until you are left on your own. I wasn't scared,
but I felt tense and I was wondering what the atmosphere
in the court was going to be like.

Surprisingly, it was not as intimidating as I thought it
would be. The room had an almost clinical atmosphere: a
large room laid out with long wooden bench tables, and
at the far end, a platform with a table for the judge. On
one side was a barred cage; up behind the judge's table a
line of arched windows were reinforced with wire mesh;
a large cross hung on the wall between them.

I walked into the court and up to a small wooden table
where I was to sit next to a translator. I don't have good
hearing in one ear and asked if I could sit with my good
ear next to the interpreter. She requested this of the judge,
and he smiled benevolently and agreed.

I looked sideways across the court, to where Amanda
Knox was sitting next to her lawyers. She was sombre
and did not make eye contact. Sollecito looked as though
he was in a daydream. It was as though he didn't know
why he was there. But I could not concentrate on looking
at them, because my attention had to be focused on the

184

questions I was to be asked. I was asked by the prosecutor, Mr Mignini, how I had found out about Meredith's death, and I told them the story of being in the bank, getting the telephone call from Arline, and scrabbling through the various foreign desks at the newspapers I knew to find out if it was Meredith who had been killed. I was also requested to give details of the kinds of things that Meredith and I enjoyed doing together, which I supplied, telling them all about the musicals and shows and films we had been to, and about the music and books that we had discussed. I also mentioned that when she was seventeen years old she had trained in karate for a year, obtaining her third belt, and that if attacked she would definitely have fought back. They asked me about whether she and Amanda had got on well, and I told the court that Meredith had often complained of Amanda Knox's hygiene habits. At this point, I looked towards Amanda, but once more there was no eye contact between us.

Having returned to our hotel for dinner, the next day we went back to court for a few hours in the morning, to listen to some of the DNA evidence concerning the alleged murder weapon – the knife – and Meredith's bra clasp, which was being presented by the prosecution and disputed by the defence lawyers. It seemed to us that progress was being made in favour of the prosecution, though we could not be sure. All along, we had said that we had faith in the Italian justice system, and that was still the case.

Dr Patrizia Stefanoni, the specialist forensics expert

from Rome who had been responsible for the original testing on the knife and bra clasp, had taken the stand. She was assured as she presented her findings. When defence lawyers told the court that contamination might have taken place during the collection of the DNA evidence, she told the court that there was no possibility of contamination in transit to the laboratory, where the tests were conducted, and that there had not been a single instance of contamination in her laboratory for at least seven years. She told the court that every precaution had been taken to ensure that different traces were not mixed.

'In collecting traces of blood stains,' she said, 'it is crucial for the operator not to come into contact with them, not to alter the scene and to avoid being infected by bacteria and viruses. Therefore, we use special gloves, boots, masks and overalls.'

Meanwhile, Sarah Gino, a geneticist brought in by the defence lawyers, challenged that regarding the DNA on the knife: 'The sample that tested positive for Meredith Kercher's DNA was so small that it had to be amplified much more than normal.'

But Dr Stefanoni explained: 'If the blood evidence is a positive match, it is not always important how much there is. And the material on the blade matched that of the victim.'

She also explained that contamination during the collection phase would not have been possible, as the forensic team that found the knife in Raffaele Sollecito's apartment was different from the one that searched the cottage. Meredith's DNA, therefore, could not have been transferred to the knife.

It was made clear that Patrizia Stefanoni had not stated that Meredith's DNA was extracted 500 times from the knife sample, but that the DNA was extracted 50 times from Meredith's sample, and was then used to compare it with other biological traces, including the one found on the knife. Even a fraction of DNA, the court was told, is unique to every individual.

As we sat in the courtroom, various displays portraying the graphs of DNA were shown on a large screen, but they meant little to us. Being ignorant of this area of scientific knowledge, it was frustrating. Sollecito's statement that Meredith had been pricked by the knife whilst he was cooking for Meredith and Amanda was also disproved, as Meredith had never been to Sollecito's home.

For the defence, DNA consultant Adriano Tagliabracci testified as to the possible contamination on the bra clasp found in Meredith's bedroom, claiming that incorrect procedures had been followed. He alleged that, in his opinion, the work of the police forensic experts was not in line with what is recommended by international bodies. He illustrated this with the fact that forty-seven days had elapsed between the discovery of Meredith's body and the retrieval of the bra clasp, and that during successive visits to the cottage the possibility of contamination increased.

Earlier, Francesco Maresca had recommended that we employ the services of two genetic and forensic experts, both for our civil case and also to back up the forensic analyses supplied by the prosecution. It was an expensive exercise for us, but we agreed to this suggestion as we knew it could be invaluable in determining what truly happened to Meredith. Although they were expensive, we personally had to pay for these consultants.

One of these consultants, Professor Francesca Torricelli, a geneticist, took the stand and said that she believed that samples of Sollecito's DNA found on Meredith's bra clasp were a significant amount, and that they were unlikely to have been left by contamination.

The head of the DNA unit of the scientific police (who are responsible for forensics), Dr Renato Biondo, and our own DNA expert Professor Torricelli, said that the information was accurate and reliable.

Similarly, Patrizia Stefanoni argued that the contamination of Meredith's bra clasp would not have been possible. DNA, she argued, is not easy to transfer. She said: 'DNA transference must not be taken for granted, nor is it is easy to happen, and more likely to take place if the original trace is aqueous, not dry.'

The bra clasp, it seemed, had been found under the pillow on 2 November, during the first search, but not collected until 18 December by a different team because it had been accidentally shifted across the bedroom and remained hidden until it was rediscovered by forensic investigators six weeks later. But the crime scene had been sealed off during that time, which greatly reduced the chances of it having been contaminated through coming into contact with other items.

The question was raised by the prosecution as to where Sollecito's DNA could have come from, if indeed there had been contamination, but his defence lawyers were never able to answer this.

As we sat in court, there was much dispute about the way in which Meredith had died, with Carlos Torre, for the defence, stating that the wound patterns on Meredith meant that a smaller knife was used for the final blow that killed her, rather than the larger knife that the prosecution was presenting to the court. 'It was done with a blade of 8 cm, which was partially extracted and plunged in at least three times,' he stated.

Information like this was extremely disturbing for Arline, Stephanie and me to hear, even through the buffer of a translator. It was one thing to know that Meredith had been stabbed, but to have to hear such graphic details was obviously upsetting.

As the size of the wound was so large, Carlos Torre argued, a repeated partial in-and-out action of the smaller knife, rather than blows from the larger kitchen knife with a blade of 16 cm found in Sollecito's kitchen, must have been responsible. He also testified that the final blow occurred whilst Meredith was lying on her back, and that there were signs of three aggressors, and that Meredith could not have cried out after the stab wound.

However, Torre conceded under cross-examination by

the prosecution that a wound the size of the larger knife was also present. This, I thought, seemed to be a self-contradiction. On the one hand Torre was saying that the larger knife was not used, and then he was saying that it was instrumental in the killing.

The dispute continued in court as to the position that Meredith was in at the time she was attacked and killed. The prosecution team had presented extensive evidence that the bruise patterns and cut marks indicated that Meredith was kneeling face down at the time, and that they all pointed to her having three attackers rather than one, who would have to have been wielding two knives with only one hand free to both hold her and to inflict bruises all over her body. Listening to this was incredibly hard and I tried to keep myself detached from the awful details I was hearing. Even though I realised that having all of this information presented was necessary, it did not make having to listen to it any easier, and I had to rein myself in from imagining it too deeply.

The idea that Meredith had more than one attacker seemed to make logical sense to me. How could one person, I wondered, restrain her in such a way as to inflict bruises all over her body, as well as make all those cuts, hold two different-sized knives, attempt to sexually assault her, and at the same time also use strangulation as a method of restraint? It would, I reasoned, have been practically impossible, and this was the prosecution's argument too.

Our other private consultant, Professor Gianaristade

Norelli, testified that the multiple lesions on Meredith's body were consistent with her having being held and attacked by more than one person. He said that she had died of suffocation and interpreted her stab wounds as having being inflicted as threats during a struggle.

The wounds, mostly on the side of the neck, were possibly inflicted by two different knives, but he noted that one of the stab wounds was compatible with the alleged murder weapon – that being the kitchen knife from Sollecito's apartment.

Professor Norelli also said that the suffocation had been caused by haemorrhaging following the neck wound, which was also aided manually by forcing the victim's mouth and nose shut, and by strangling her. This, Norelli said, showed a clear intent to kill, while the neck wounds might have been inflicted with the intent to scare and threaten the victim.

There were also contradictions between the defence teams themselves. Whilst Carlos Torre had stated that Meredith had been killed from the front, Francesco Intona, Sollecito's forensic expert, said that she had been killed from behind. The debate rested on the fact that there was no biological material under Meredith's finger-nails, which there would have been if she had been fighting back if attacked from the front.

Soon after this graphic breakdown of the last moments of Meredith's life, we left the court and returned to our hotel. There was nothing more that we could do here, in Perugia, where my daughter had gone to die. We felt drained by the trip, and home was still a long way away.

As a final straw, we soon learned that we would not be able to get to the airport in Rome in time for our return flight, as our journey would involve changing trains, and the only connection we could get would make us miss the departure time. As fortune would have it, an off-duty police driver offered to take us on the two-hour journey there by road – though we would have to pay for this trip, at least we would be on our way home.

Sitting together in the airport lounge, we all knew that we would have to return to Perugia in the winter to hear the verdict on Knox and Sollecito delivered by Judge Massei and the jury. Exactly when we would have to return was uncertain, but we knew that it would be some months before we received any notification. As we lifted our bags and listened out for our boarding call, none of us was any the wiser as to which way the verdict would go. All we wanted was justice for Meredith.

8

The Verdict

While we tried to go on having normal lives in England, the trial of Amanda Knox and Raffaele Sollecito continued in Perugia. Their defence lawyers continued to argue that contamination could have taken place on the alleged murder weapon and Meredith's bra clasp, points they were to pursue not only throughout the trial, but throughout the appeal process as well.

As the conclusion of the trial approached, with all witnesses having been heard and all the evidence having been presented to the court, the defence lawyers for Sollecito and Knox requested that an independent review of the DNA evidence and forensic findings be considered by the court.

In response to this request, the prosecutor, Giuliano Mignini, said: 'There is no need for a review, as the evidence was gathered in a very professional way by qualified persons.'

It took the two judges and the six-person jury two hours of deliberation before rejecting the request. As

Judge Massei explained: 'The court has heard from various consultants who brought several elements to the case, and which rule out the need for any further proof.'

Amanda Knox's lawyer, Luciano Ghirga, responded: 'This doesn't change anything. We wanted to clarify the evidence, but obviously the judge doesn't feel that he needs additional information. We are ready to argue.'

Just after the request was rejected, Edda Mellas appeared on the Larry King show in America. There, she said: 'We asked for an independent review because we were sure that anyone who looked at it would support us.' Perhaps optimistically, she then went on to add: 'Maybe the court has decided that they didn't need that support; that our argument was good enough.'

Our lawyer impressed upon us that the decision to reject the independent review was not meant to be interpreted as a presumption of innocence or guilt. As he commented: 'We all know that in all trials of this nature, there are different analyses of forensic evidence made by the various expert witnesses. The court must now consider the seriousness and integrity of the experts' testimony.'

The defence lawyers also challenged the prosecution's argument that there were multiple attackers, arguing that it would not have been possible for there to have been four people in Meredith's small bedroom at the time of her murder. Our lawyer pointed out that when the jury had visited Meredith's room, there were seven people in there.

* * *

In England, my family and I knew that we were going to return to Perugia for the final verdict, which we had been told would probably be in the December of 2009. Yet, by now, we had already made several vital trips to Perugia, and every one of them drained us financially. When the time came to hear the verdict, we all wanted to be there, but we were struggling to find the necessary funds to finance the journey. A single trip with flights, hotel, transport and other expenses could come to several thousand pounds, and none of us had that kind of money in reserve.

We found it surprising that there was a complete lack of financial support from the British Government. We had received tremendous support from the British Consulate in Florence, who arranged for translation facilities when we were dealing with the Italian authorities, and made transport arrangements, but despite our pleas, we had not received any financial support from the Foreign Office. A number of MPs campaigned on our behalf for some form of contribution towards our flights, but every time their efforts were to no avail. Indeed, it seemed that this was a policy decision, one that did not affect just us, but anybody who suffered such an ordeal as my family and I had. In response to their requests, the MPs seemed to receive simple catch-all denials:

Thank you for your letter to the Foreign Secretary about what Government assistance is available to victims of crimes and their families overseas. Our primary concern for British nationals who have been a victim of crime overseas is their welfare. If they have been hospitalised, we can visit them. We can provide a list of English-speaking lawyers and interpreters and a list of doctors and medical facilities, if appropriate. But we do not provide emergency financial help to victims of crimes abroad. We cannot pay bills, and we cannot give British nationals money. In certain circumstances, and when everything else has been tried, we might provide a loan from public funds, but this will need to be paid back. We do not meet the costs of relatives to attend court hearings overseas.

This was despite the fact that we were obliged to provide testimonies in court.

Nor could we expect any help from the Italian Government. Sometime before Meredith was murdered, the EU states had all agreed to sign an agreement that they would compensate the families of any foreign nationals who had become victims of a violent crime committed in their country. However, of all the EU states, Italy failed to sign the agreement in time. Financially, we were alone – and though this was a small burden compared to what we had been through, it made the business of attending the trial, and seeking justice for Meredith, all the more problematic.

As the trial approached its conclusion, I was becoming increasingly disturbed at the way Amanda Knox, nick-named 'Foxy Knoxy' by the media, had acquired an almost celebrity status. Raffaele Sollecito's role in the case seemed to have been deliberately neglected, to allow more space for stories about Amanda Knox, including lurid details about her private life. And just as Sollecito seemed to have been sidelined, so too had Meredith been relegated to the fringes of her own story. This was a particularly painful burden to bear. It was Meredith whose life had been taken, Meredith who had gone to Perugia never to return home, Meredith for whom we were all seeking justice – and yet the press seemed to be much more concerned about what fashions Amanda Knox was wearing in court.

Almost every press item that appeared seemed to concentrate on Knox, and I felt that something had to be done to redress the balance. As a journalist all my adult life, I knew there were avenues I could follow to make sure the focus was, in some way, shifted back to Meredith, and I wrote an article to express these exact feelings for the *Daily Mail*. Judging by comments I read online, the article seemed to gain some support, both here and abroad, and it was a consolation of sorts to know that we were not the only ones who felt this way. Our family agreed that the focus had shifted from Meredith, who was the victim, and that was upsetting. She deserved so much more than that.

On 20 November 2009, the prosecutor began his summing-up in court, a short while after the second anniversary of Meredith's murder.

In a dramatic seven-hour presentation, which included the showing of an animated video demonstrating the prosecution's allegations as to how the murder of Meredith had evolved and been committed, Giuliano Mignini portrayed Amanda Knox as a person bent on revenge against her housemate.

Outlining the prosecution's scenario, he claimed that Meredith was already at home when Amanda Knox, Raffaele Sollecito and Rudy Guede had arrived. It was assumed by the prosecution that Meredith had already discovered that the 300 euros she had withdrawn from her bank to pay the rent were missing. During the initial stages of the investigation it had been suggested that the rent money Meredith had withdrawn, and which she had discovered was missing on her return home, might have been the cause of an argument between Knox and Meredith.

As translated by Italian lawyers and reproduced on the True Justice for Meredith Kercher website, Mr Mignini said:

'Meredith and Amanda began to argue over money. Meredith was also upset that Amanda had brought another man [Guede] back to the house. They argued about this ugly habit of hers, and the three who had arrived were also under the influence of drugs and possibly alcohol.

'Meredith was far too serious a girl for her. Amanda didn't like her. She didn't like her friends, because they were critical of hygiene and habits. Amanda had developed

Stephanie, Meredith and Arline. This photo was taken when Meredith was still studying at Leeds University.

Meredith and Arline together celebrating Arline's birthday, the year before she left for Perugia.

Meredith had no idea
how lovely she was.

Meredith holding her
certificate for passing
her first year.

Meredith and her
friend Flick at
Leeds University.

Meredith out enjoying herself shortly before she was killed.

The order of service from Meredith's funeral.

The people of Perugia have taken Meredith into their hearts and were devastated by what happened.

The message I left for her.

Arline, Stephanie and I lighting a candle for Meredith.

The cottage where Meredith lived. She chose it because she loved the view.

Perugia's University for Foreigners, where Meredith fought to study.

Perugia is a beautiful medieval town.

Stephanie, Arline and I on that first terrible trip to Perugia.

Lyle, me, Stephanie and Arline enter the court.

The press attention has been enormous, and at times difficult to cope with.

Facing the cameras.

The media gathering
to hear the appeal
verdict.

The family giving
a press conference
following the
acquittal of Knox
and Sollecito.

Tributes to our beautiful girl.

a deep hatred for Meredith and, that night, the time had come for her to take revenge. Amanda grabbed her by the hair and hit her head on the floor or the wall. Sollecito was threatening her with a knife and Rudy Guede was finishing his sexual assault.

'Amanda also had a knife, and held it to the left side of Kercher's throat and, as the crescendo of violence grew, she inflicted the deepest cut. Meredith did not want to submit to sexual violence.'

Mignini also suggested that Sollecito and Guede were competing for Knox's attention. 'The key to the mystery is in the room where the supposed break-in took place,' he added. 'It would have been manna from heaven for Amanda and Sollecito if blood or other genetic evidence from an unknown party had been found on the broken glass or window frame. But nothing was found.

'This hypothetical thief then did something quite remarkable. He didn't take anything of value. No jewellery was missing. Computers were left at the scene, as well as designer bags and clothes. A "very strange break-in" was, in fact, how the first police officer who arrived at the house described it. They could not believe that nothing of value was taken.'

The deputy prosecutor, Manuela Comodi, took the stand the following day, speaking of the DNA and forensic evidence. 'In every biological analysis, the risk of deterioration and contamination is inherent. Patrizia Stefanoni, the biologist of the scientific police, has, however, put in action all of the due procedures to avoid these phenomena, and nobody can affirm the contrary. The consultants for the parties, then, took part in all the inspection and analyses.'

The prosecution went on to outline a chronology of events as they saw it.

On 1 November, Meredith leaves the house at Via della Pergola to have dinner with her friends. Later, Amanda Knox leaves Sollecito's apartment;, at around 6 p.m., he watches the film *Amélie*.

Knox receives a text from Patrick Lumumba, owner of the bar Le Chic, to tell her that she is not required to work that evening. At around 8.30 p.m., she returns to Sollecito's home and, about a quarter of an hour later, Sollecito turns off his mobile phone.

Having enjoyed a dinner with friends, Meredith walks home with her friend Sophie Purton at about 9 p.m., continuing the second half her journey alone. Meredith enters her house and settles down, alone, to do some university work.

At approximately 9.45 p.m., Knox and Sollecito leave his apartment and go to Piazza Grimana, where they set up an observation on the house where Meredith is alone. They rendezvous with Rudy Guede, and almost one and a half hours later, they enter the house using Knox's key.

On entering the house, Guede goes to the bathroom and the argument between Meredith and Knox ensues. Knox grabs Meredith by the hair and slams her into the wardrobe. The scuffle is helped by Sollecito.

Guede enters the room and joins in, whereupon he commences his sexual assault on Meredith. After Meredith has been struck by the knife, which leads to her agonising death, Knox and Sollecito leave the house, taking Meredith's mobile phones with them, so that she cannot ring for help. Guede then gets towels from the bathroom, using them to try to stem the flow of blood from Meredith's neck wound.

On their flight, Knox and Sollecito throw Meredith's phones into the garden in Via Sperandio. They return to the house at some point during the night or in the early hours of 2 November to clean up the evidence and stage the fake burglary.

Giuliano Mignini and Manuela Comodi completed their summing-up by requesting of the judge and jury that Knox and Sollecito be sentenced to life imprisonment. Mr Mignini added that Knox should serve nine months of her sentence in day isolation, while Sollecito should serve two months of his sentence under the same conditions.

We learned all of these details in England through our lawyer, who informed us that we were to fly out to Perugia for the verdict on 4 December. It was a nervous time for us, not knowing what the verdict might be, whether they would be found guilty of the crime or be found innocent and instantly released. We debated the evidence that had been presented in the court between ourselves, and though we felt that it pointed towards a guilty verdict, we knew that this was a decision only the judge and jury could make.

When all of our family arrived in Perugia and took a taxi to our hotel, we learned that the jury were still deliberating and that the verdict might not come through until two the following morning. Whereas throughout the trial the jury members had been allowed home, once the trial ended and deliberations began, they were obliged to remain at the courthouse until a decision had been reached. No one had any idea how long this would take.

We sat in the reception area to the dining room of our hotel with our lawyer. When the court was ready, he would receive a call and tell us that it was time to assemble there. Especially after all the travelling we had done, it was a long, exhausting wait. In the end, we resolved that we had time to have dinner, so we took ourselves to the hotel restaurant for some food. It was a peculiar time, and it seemed as if none of us knew what to say. Back in the foyer, we continued our long wait. Our lawyer and others had no idea which way the jury would go. We waited and we waited.

It was approaching midnight when our lawyer's mobile phone rang. 'That's it,' he said, finishing his conversation.

Eyeing each other silently, we climbed into the waiting police cars and were escorted to the courthouse.

The press outside were manic, clambering over each other to get pictures of us. Inside the court, they were hanging over a balcony; as we entered the court itself, more press clamoured behind a rail, awaiting the verdict.

Surprisingly, like our own lawyer, none of the prosecutors or defence lawyers was in ceremonial garb. Instead, they stood around chatting to each other wearing regular suits.

Amanda Knox and Raffaele Sollecito were led into the court under a heavily armed guard of police and conducted to their seats by their respective lawyers. Although Knox looked nervous, Sollecito had that same blank and indifferent expression he had worn throughout the proceedings, as though he had no idea why he was there.

Then someone indicated that Judge Massei was about to enter. Almost instantaneously, the prosecutor, our lawyer and the defence lawyers pulled on their legal robes. What had at first looked like an informal gathering, suddenly turned into an austere and sombre congregation. The gentle hum of conversation that had pervaded the room suddenly evaporated. We were in complete silence.

We sat to the rear and left of the court, near the door through which we had entered, an official interpreter at our side. The head of Homicide, Monica Napoleone, was seated in front of me.

At long last, Judge Massei entered the court. From where we were sitting, he looked a million miles away, and when he began speaking, it was in a soft and quiet voice that even if I had understood Italian, I doubt I would have heard.

I looked towards Amanda Knox and Raffaele Sollecito: gone was the confidence and smile that Knox had displayed throughout the pretrial and trial. Then, as the judge delivered his pronouncement, in an Italian I could not understand, I watched her collapsing forwards. I saw her parents' look of disbelief.

Still, I had no idea what this meant. Had Knox pitched forward in relief, or was it devastation? Had she and Sollecito been released? Was the long wait to find justice for Meredith going to go on even longer?

Our interpreter turned to us, and it was only then that I understood what had happened in the courtroom. Knox and Sollecito had been found guilty of Meredith's murder. Amanda Knox had been sentenced to twenty-six years in prison, which included one year for implicating an innocent man in the crime; Sollecito had been given twenty-five years behind bars.

Knox seemed totally distraught, but again, Sollecito seemed to be in a dreamworld, completely unaware of what had just been said.

Behind us, some members of the press were crying. I had no idea whether it was because they thought that justice had been done or because they believed they had just witnessed a terrible miscarriage of justice. Some even seemed unable to use their cameras.

Our family was still seated by the entrance door when Amanda Knox was led from the court, held by police. She was crying and crumpled, and even though I was feeling that justice had been done, it was not a pleasant sight. I did not feel any elation. Even now, I cannot put into words exactly what I felt. For more than two years now I had wondered what my reaction was going to be to this moment, but, in fact, I did not seem to have any reaction at all. For me, there was only a deep and unsettling numbness, as if I was far away. I looked at Amanda Knox, and all I could think was that there, standing in front of me, was the young woman who had been found guilty of my daughter's murder. There was not any pandemonium in the court. If anything there was a heavy silence, lawyers moving and talking to each other quietly.

Amanda Knox disappeared through the door. After she was gone, Sollecito followed, again with that bewildered expression on his face. The whole process of the verdict had lasted less than ten minutes. In the middle of it all, I sat there, thinking that I was in some strange world, that none of this was truly happening. Two years of wondering what was going to happen had reached some kind of conclusion, and yet it did not feel as if we had come to the end of any road, only that the road went on and on. Already, I knew that appeals were going to follow. Today's verdict was only another step on that long, lonely road. It started with Meredith's murder, but it would not end.

Monica Napoleone and other police officers took my family and me down a corridor and a flight of stairs to an exit at the rear of the court. Monica gripped my arm tightly and protectively. I dreaded that there was going to be an army of press awaiting us, but to my eternal relief there were no photographers. I have no idea what the scene was like at the front of the court. I imagine that it was pandemonium, as the flashbulbs lit up the night air. Yet, for once, we were able to escape without running the gauntlet of press and photographers.

In the police cars we sat in silence, not able to summon any words to speak about what had happened in court. Slowly, we wound our way through the streets back towards our hotel. Around us there were no people, only the darkness of the night. Perugia seemed still and serene, peaceful perhaps.

We were all exhausted, but sleep would not come to me that night. That night we could not discuss the verdicts; it seemed there was nothing left to say. Certainly, there was nothing that could change a single second of what had happened since that November night. We raised our glasses to Meredith again, and then long, sleepless hours stretched ahead. Once we had said our goodnights, I stood at my hotel bedroom window and stared at the lights of houses in the distance, scattered on the horizon. I wanted to feel relief, to feel *something*, but the only relief I could muster was that we did not have to deliver a press conference that night. There had been enough drama for today.

The next morning, we knew we would have to face the media, and we agreed to provide a press conference at our hotel. Together, my family and I entered a room that was packed with more than eighty photographers and about fifteen television film crews. They had come from England and America, as well as Italy, and I wondered what was left to say.

John, Lyle, Stephanie, Arline and I sat at a long table, flanked by our lawyer, Francesco Maresca, and an interpreter from the British Embassy in Rome. Photographers clambered over each other to place microphones on our table, and the rest were crammed shoulder to shoulder, seated and standing in front of us.

I noticed a young Italian woman photographer trying to get an angled shot of me and I looked at her. She smiled appreciatively. It was a strange experience. We had been through too many press conferences already, but this time it felt different somehow. This was not about predictions or expectations; this was about a real verdict that the court had come to, and so the questions were obviously going to be more direct. I was staggered at how many photographs the press could take. The flash of bulbs seemed never to end. Men looked down their cameras at us as though looking through telescopes.

My children are much more confident and eloquent than I am in these situations, and when Lyle was asked whether we were elated at the verdict he replied: 'Ultimately, we are pleased with the decision and that we got a decision. But at the end of the day, it is not a time for triumph or celebration. We are satisfied. But we are gathered here because our sister was murdered and brutally taken away from us, and all of our lives and everyone who knew her, and people around the world who didn't, have been touched by it. But two young people have been sentenced to a long time behind bars, and the other gentleman was a year ago.'

Asked what she felt about the judge and jury's decision, Arline said: 'The evidence has been presented and you have to agree with that verdict.'

As a result of the verdict, the judge had awarded our family millions of euros in compensation, as had been requested by our lawyer at an earlier stage in the trial. This was not for any kind of monetary satisfaction on our behalf, and we knew that we would never get a penny of it. When asked about it, Lyle replied to the press: 'The compensation that we have been awarded as part of our civil case [which had run concurrently with that of the prosecution] is not of the same meaning as it would be in the United Kingdom. Here, in Italy, you request it because it is more to emphasise the severity of the case and add weight, to show the gravity of the case.

'I'm certain that many people would imagine, when they see the amount of 20 million euros being touted about, that any sane person would say that, clearly, if you were putting in for any compensation, you wouldn't put in for an amount like that. It's not a case of us seeking any money, hence we have been reluctant to do much media stuff throughout. Money won't change anything in that respect.'

Indeed, we have never received a penny in compensation for Meredith's murder.

Meredith's brother John, said: 'Meredith still leaves a big hole in our lives, and her presence is missed every time that we meet up as a family. Everyone in the room here associates Meredith with a tragic event, but we would prefer not to remember her in that way. So we would like to concentrate on the twenty-one years that we had with her.'

Stephanie spoke up: 'But we are very lucky that we have a lot of memories of her, and we learn more about Meredith from her friends, and that way she is still very much a part of our lives and always will be.'

Trying to evaluate what had happened, Arline told the assembled press: 'We are the ones who have been given a life sentence. We have to live with what's happened, for the rest of our lives. People say that time heals, but it doesn't.'

Lyle added: 'Being angry won't bring Meredith back. I was shocked when the verdict came in. You don't know how to feel.'

This was precisely how I had felt at that moment in the court.

Stephanie told the press, as they thrust their microphones in front of her: 'People always ask us about Amanda Knox and Raffaele Sollecito, but it's not our place to judge them. That's what the judges and jury were there for. We can only go on the evidence that we heard; what we've been told about their behaviour, and what they did.'

Our interpreter from the British Embassy signalled to the press that we had said all we could and they accepted that. As we made our way through their ranks, they were respectful and non-intrusive. They had their comments, the pictures, their news footage, and I could see them packing away their cameras.

Yet for us, there was still one more thing to do before we made our way back to England. An Italian television station had put in a request for us to do an interview with them. I was somewhat reluctant about this as I had always declined any television interviews. We had, from the beginning, been inundated with requests from American and British television networks, and I had always declined – but, on this occasion, I relented. I knew there would be huge attention focused on Amanda Knox and Raffaele Sollecito and it felt important to me to speak about Meredith.

We were shown into a small hotel suite where the film and sound people were stationed, and there we met a young female television presenter. I explained that I did not want us to have to answer any questions regarding Knox and Sollecito, or the trial, and they respected this. Most of the questions directed to us were concerned with Meredith, which I did not mind answering. They asked me what Meredith had been like as a person, what kind of things we enjoyed doing together. Surprisingly, I was not as nervous about doing this as I had anticipated. Everything was fine, and the whole event only took about half an hour.

At last, it was time for us to return to England. We were driven to the airport and, of course, there was a small press presence awaiting us. For the first time, it did not feel as intimidating as it had done before. We waited for our flight, almost in silence. There did not seem to be anything we wanted to talk about, not too much for us to say to each other at this stage.

Did this verdict represent some sort of 'closure' for us, a term that so many people had used? If I thought about it closely, I had to accept that it didn't. We were well aware that, under Italian law, the convicted had two rights of appeal. Firstly, they would be able to appeal their convictions to the Perugian court that had convicted them; if that failed, they would have recourse to the Supreme Court in Rome. This could take at least a year, if not longer. With the potential for these appeals still hanging over us, we did not have the closure that we would have liked. We were only at the first stage of a long legal process, and things in Italy progress at a slower pace than in some other Western countries.

Aboard the plane, we wondered what the next stage would be. We knew that there would be long passages of silence with nothing happening, as the defence lawyers prepared their respective cases for their appeals. This, we understood, was not something that would occur in a few weeks. It would take months before we knew what was happening. Our lawyer had also told us that Judge Massei would have to prepare a report to be publicly published, outlining the reasons exactly why he and the jury had chosen to convict Knox and Sollecito. This was to be quite a long process, as every precise detail had to be included, and he had up to ninety days to deliver it.

As our flight landed at Stansted, a member of the airport staff approached us to say that there were press waiting for us in the arrivals area. There was nothing we could do about it, except to brave it one final time and walk through them. The flashbulbs went off, there were questions fired at us, but we really had nothing to say. We had said enough already, and now all we wanted was some peace.

With the verdict having been delivered so late at night, the story could not be carried in the morning newspapers. That would have to wait for the following day. But the television stations were carrying it as their leading news story. On screen, segments of the press conference that we had given were repeated time and time again. Then the telephones started ringing: American and British television networks wanting us to appear on their programmes; newspapers requesting interviews; magazine shows wanting us to appear. We politely declined all of them, but the pressure continued throughout the next day too, and by then it was front-page news on every newspaper.

Occasionally, a reporter would arrive at the house where Arline lived, but she had to tell them that there was nothing more that we could say and, thankfully, they accepted that.

As a family, we were still shaky about the events that we had been through, and for days afterwards we were extremely tired. Even if we had wanted to, we could not turn around and say 'So that's it,' because it wasn't. Even amongst ourselves, we could hardly find the words to express what we were feeling. We had all been there, we had all gone through it – somehow, that seemed to be enough. It was a feeling I could not put into words, but one I knew we all shared.

Before the verdict had been delivered, I had struggled in my own mind to predict what the outcome would be; it had been impossible to envisage. There was no way that, having lived through what we had lived through, we could have any idea what the jury might have been thinking. Sometimes, I can still see myself sitting at the back of the court, Knox and Sollecito in the room, waiting and waiting for the verdict to be delivered, watching the reactions and looks of disbelief before our interpreter could turn to us and tell us what had happened.

But now, back home, I imagined myself staring out of the living-room window of my first-floor flat in Croydon to see Meredith standing on the other side of the road in her school uniform, waiting to cross. I heard her laugh, saw her smile, remembered the professionalism she displayed when, years later, as a university student, she had poured drinks in the restaurant she had worked in to raise some money for her studies. I saw her as an eight-year-old in Italy, eating pizza and drinking iced tea on the beach in the Italian resort of Rimini. And, most of all, I heard her singing Whitney Houston's song 'I Will Always Love You' to me on my answerphone as a twelve-year-old. I can still hear her voice. You can't take memories like that away, and they are going to be with me for ever.

When we spoke together, as a family, we would often debate what the next step would be. We tried to work out how long the appeals of Amanda Knox and Raffaele Sollecito would take. We did not anticipate that it would be almost two years before the result of that appeal would be announced. Meanwhile, messages of support flooded in on the Internet, quite a few written to Meredith herself. In a way, she lived on through those messages, and how powerfully she seemed to have touched people around the world.

Two and a half weeks later, after the verdict, it was Christmas Day. Then, on 28 December, it was Meredith's birthday. She would have been twenty-four years old. Our family and a few of Meredith's friends went to the cemetery on both occasions to leave her flowers and cards. I wished her 'Happy Birthday, wherever you are.' I blew her a kiss.

I looked down at the stones and flowers on her grave and I thought, You never deserved this.

More than ever, I wanted justice for her.

9

The Appeal

The convictions of Amanda Knox and Raffaele Sollecito seemed to have international repercussions, the like of which I had not anticipated. Following their sentencing, the outcry from certain quarters of America could be heard across the world, and was reported widely. Much of this criticism seemed to focus on the hypothetical idea that the trial had been anti-American in sentiment, and implied that the conviction of an American citizen in Italy had more to do with political thinking than it did with innocence or guilt. At home in Croydon, I struggled to understand why exactly the outcry had come about. That the trial was tainted by anti-Americanism was, to me, a ludicrous supposition, considering that Sollecito was Italian and that Guede, though African by birth, had lived in Italy for many years. Furthermore, Perugia was twinned with Seattle, the town of Amanda Knox's birth.

Senator Maria Cantwell of Washington State, of which Seattle is the capital, proposed bringing Secretary of State Hillary Clinton into the debate. Cantwell was quoted in the press as saying: 'I am saddened by the verdict, and I have serious questions about the Italian justice system, and whether anti-Americanism tainted the trial. The prosecution did not present enough evidence for an impartial jury to conclude, beyond reasonable doubt, that Ms Knox was guilty. Other flaws in the Italian justice system include . . . negligent handling of evidence by investigators. I am in contact with the US Ambassador to Italy, and have been since the time of Ms Knox's arrest. I shall be conveying my concerns to Secretary of State Hillary Clinton.'

That politicians were, after what I have always felt to be a full and fair trial, becoming involved seemed deeply unfair to me, and the fact that they were turning Meredith's murder trial into a soapbox from which to damn the Italian justice system only hardened my family's belief that Meredith was being written out of her own story. Senator Cantwell's statements felt particularly unreasonable. I wondered if she was aware, when she said that the prosecution had provided 'insufficient evidence', that they had, in fact, presented more than 10,000 pages of evidence.

Upon hearing the negative comments coming from the US, the Italian press retaliated, with the Italian newspaper *Il Messaggero* commenting: 'If there is any ground upon which our country will not be taught lessons on civility and respect from anyone, the United States included, then it is the penal process.'

Prosecutor Mignini said: 'This senator should not interfere. It is something that she has no idea about. I am happy with how the trial went.' He added: 'In my conscience, I know that I have done my duty. It is never easy to ask for a life sentence. That is especially true in this case, where the accused were in their twenties. I have three children who are more or less the same age. Asking for life was the right punishment for the crime. I am not prepared to take criticism from the Americans on how the prosecution or investigators carried out their work.'

He went on to emphasise: 'The case went before nineteen judges, in the end, at various levels from a preliminary hearing, through three levels of re-examination, and all found in the prosecution's favour.'

Even Amanda Knox's legal team were displeased with Senator Cantwell's remarks. In response to the proposal by Senator Cantwell to bring the secretary of state into the debate, Knox's lawyer Luciano Ghirga was quoted in the Italian newspapers as having said: 'That's all we need, Hillary Clinton involved. I have the same political sympathies as her. But this sort of thing does not help us in any way.'

There was also some anxiety in America itself, with a group of concerned Seattle voters feeling compelled to write to the senator to express their own feelings. The True Justice for Meredith Kercher website reported them as saying:

A number of your well-informed constituents are wondering about your motivations for suddenly injecting yourself into the Meredith Kercher trial debate, immediately following the unanimous guilty ruling for Amanda Knox in Perugia, Italy.

We wonder, because you said that you were 'saddened by the verdict', and said that you had serious questions about the Italian judicial system and whether anti-Americanism had tainted the trial. But then you went on to describe how you knew for a fact that the prosecution in the case did not present enough evidence for an impartial jury to conclude beyond reasonable doubt that Amanda Knox was guilty.

We are confused because, it seems to us, that if you had been following the case closely enough to be certain that not enough evidence had been presented by the prosecution, then you would consequently have a clear idea of how the Italian judicial system functioned and whether anti-American sentiment had impacted the ruling.

Were you aware that Raffaele Sollecito, an Italian, was convicted alongside Ms Knox, and that he received some of the best legal representation available in Italy, including senior lawyer, Giulia Bongiorno, who won fame as a criminal lawyer when she successfully defended former premier, Giulio Andreotti, a few years ago? She said nothing about anti-American sentiment having influenced the ruling against her client, nor did she complain about fundamental problems with the way that the trial was run.

Asked by the British press for her comments, Arline was keen to underline our belief that the trial had been conducted fully and fairly. As we had repeatedly said, across the course of the whole process, we trusted and had faith in the Italian justice system.

Arline said: 'As a family, we are not aware of any anti-American sentiment expressed at any stage during the trial. It was a murder trial, with three suspects, one of whom had already been convicted and sentenced. The prosecution presented its case with a large amount of evidence, and the defence for the accused had their opportunity to present their case. Two judges and a jury then had their deliberations to reach their verdict.'

I fully agreed with Arline and we discussed this at great length. Though we looked at it from every possible angle we could think of, we could not see a way in which any right-minded person might realistically believe that the trial had been anti-American. Amanda Knox herself had never raised any issue about this and nor had her lawyers.

Yet the pressure from America had mounted throughout the trial, much of it from King County in the state of Washington, whose capital is, of course, Amanda Knox's home town.

Washington State Superior Court Judge Michael Heavey was particularly pointed in his criticism. Though the True Justice for Meredith Kercher website commented that he is ordinarily recognised to be a fair commentator, I thought it curious that his daughter had gone to school with Amanda Knox and that he, therefore, may well have been familiar with her family. It began to feel as if some of Amanda Knox's supporters had created a groundswell of noise and opinion. Meanwhile, my family and I, still upset that the media frenzy was focusing on Knox, felt like we were a tiny, quiet voice crying out in the wilderness.

The *Seattle Post-Intelligencer* reported Judge Michael Heavey as saying: 'It borders on the diabolical. To me, it just shows that they don't care whether she is guilty or innocent. They just believe that Amanda needs to be convicted. When you have a heinous crime and a demonised defendant, with very little evidence, you can get a bad conviction. I haven't been sure of too much in my life, but I'm totally convinced that she is innocent.'

These comments – and Michael Heavey was far from the only one making such accusations – only made me feel that the case was not being fully and accurately reported across America, and that people there were not fully aware of all the evidence that had been presented in court.

Judge Heavey was alleged to have written to the highest authorities in Italy requesting that the trial be moved from Perugia. This was interpreted by some analysts as meaning that he wanted the trial to be transferred to America. This, apparently, was erroneous, as the request had simply been for the trial to be transferred from Perugia to another Italian location.

Anne Bremner, an attorney and legal analyst – like Heavey, also from King County – also seemed to have been 'accused' of requesting that the trial be transferred. She stated:

I did not request, and would never request, that Italy yield jurisdiction over a criminal case arising within its borders. This erroneous allegation was made by the London *Telegraph*, and they formally retracted it the next day, but not before it was widely repeated. Italy is one of the great democracies, with public institutions that befit that status. I have no doubt that the Italian court system will deliver justice in the end.

At the same time, this particular case has been managed by Perugia's chief prosecutor, Giuliano Mignini, in a way that the public should know about. Somebody needs to challenge the bizarre conjecture through which Mignini and his associates have turned a straightforward murder into a fable with no precedent in the annals of crime. And somebody needs to make the point against it, until the world understands that Amanda and Raffaele Sollecito are innocent. The case against them is based on evidence so ambiguous and compromised that it should have no place in a fair trial.

But the prosecution has done a good job of using lies, distortions and innuendo to incite resentment and public prejudice against these innocent suspects, and that is why I am speaking out. No one is paying me to do so. I have practiced law for twenty-five years, both as a prosecutor and as a defense attorney, and I recognize an outrage when I see one. This case is an outrage.

I felt that this was strong stuff. This had been a murder trial involving three suspects and three different nationalities. The prosecution had presented a large amount of evidence and the defence had had their consultants to make their refutations. Yet again, it felt as if an American media machine had swung into action, and I began to worry deeply about what effect it would have.

In the autumn of 2009, during the trial, the television newscaster Larry King had interviewed Amanda Knox's biological parents, Curt Knox and Edda Mellas on CNN News. King has always been a respected, Emmy Award-winning broadcaster, but in this interview – in which Knox's parents were joined by video link with respected New York lawyer John Q. Kelly – he seemed to show a benign attitude, without his trademark challenging questions. Watching it unfold felt rather peculiar. I was familiar with Larry King's style, but this seemed, to me, to be a one-sided presentation, without any balance and with little reference to the facts established in court. I was surprised to see that King offered no probing questions, and the whole show seemed, to me, to be a simple opportunity for Curt Knox and Edda Mellas to say their piece.

I was equally baffled by the lawyer John Q. Kelly's statements. Kelly, I learned, was known for his fairness to victims in murder cases – but, as far as I was concerned, he presented an appalling desertion of the facts that had emerged in the trial in Perugia.

He said: 'There's no forensic evidence, there's no physical evidence. There's no substantive evidence against Amanda. I think that the only forensic evidence that they had was a small portion of Amanda's DNA on the knife in Raffaele's apartment, where she was, all of the time. And it's not even consistent with the weapon that was used.'

Listening to these comments, I was astounded that Kelly seemed completely ignorant of or oblivious to the facts. In fact, the prosecution had presented compelling evidence to say that Amanda's footprints, mixed with Meredith's blood, had been found in the hallway outside Meredith's room, and also that her footprint had been found in the room belonging to her Italian housemate Filomena Romanelli, where the prosecution had said a burglary had been staged. Kelly also seemed to be oblivious to the fact that Amanda's DNA had been found mixed with Meredith's in three separate locations in the bathroom.

As to the knife, it had already been established that two knives seemed to have been used in the attack, and even an expert for the defence had admitted in court that one of the wounds on Meredith's neck was consistent with the larger knife, on which Amanda's DNA had been found.

Forensic expert Patrizia Stefanoni had also testified in court that all of the tests performed on the larger knife were conducted properly, and that there was no risk of contamination during the conducting of these tests.

Kelly could have been justified in questioning the validity of evidence presented by the prosecution – this is, after all, the right of every defence lawyer – but to state that there was 'no forensic evidence linking Amanda Knox' or, indeed, Raffaele Sollecito to the scene was to ignore the basic facts.

However, speaking to Larry King, Kelly further said: 'My thoughts, Larry: it's probably the most international railroading of two innocent young people that I have ever seen. This is actually a public lynching based on rank speculation and vindictiveness. It's just a nightmare what these parents are going through, and what these young adults are going through too.'

I was angered by his comments, because there was no mention of Meredith or the nightmare that we had suffered, and continued to suffer. How could Kelly really say that the Italian justice system was being 'vindictive', when all that was being done was what would be done under any justice system, namely the presenting of a large body of evidence that, in the opinion of the prosecution, linked the suspects to the crime?

I was also puzzled why neither King nor Kelly made no reference to Rudy Guede. Guede's conviction, which had been conducted separately from the trial of Knox and Sollecito, did not seem to figure in anybody's thoughts – and, significantly, nobody cared to address the question of *who* exactly might have committed the crime alongside Guede, if Knox and Sollecito were truly innocent. It had already been established, by various expert witnesses, that Meredith must have had more than one assailant, something that my family and I had instinctively felt from the outset.

Having studied criminology for several years for my degree at London University, I felt that what all these legal commentators were forgetting was that it does not matter what evidence the prosecution has presented; the defence has the right, as in any democratic legal process, to challenge that evidence, and the final verdict is delivered by an impartial jury. At least, I reasoned, Knox's and Sollecito's defence lawyers had worked on disproving the evidence; these commentators, in no way connected with the trial, were simply ignoring that it existed.

Speaking in the same televised interview with Larry King, Amanda Knox's father, Curt Knox, said: 'I believe that there was a huge mistake made early on by police, making it a closed-case presentation by the police, and when they found out that Rudy Guede was the one who actually did it, they were too far into it, and I've been trying to press it ever since.'

What I found even more disconcerting were the personal verbal attacks from America levelled at Perugia's chief prosecutor, Giuliano Mignini. Some of these attacks were so concerted that even the defence lawyers expressed their concern at the treatment being accorded to a highly respected individual. Lawyers from both sides of the trial, it seemed, resented 'interference' from America.

In an interview, Mignini told the BBC that one Seattle-based newspaper had reported comments that he was 'mentally unstable'. 'These are allegations from 9,000 kilometres away,' he said, 'from people who have no knowledge of me and to whom I have never spoken. I am quite a healthy man. I don't go to the doctor much, and I have never visited a psychologist.'

It was also suggested by supporters of Knox that Mignini had leaked information from the prosecutor's office, when in fact everything had been openly discussed in court. The media seemed to want to turn the trial into an arena full of scandal, sleaze, corruption and gossip – and my family and I began to wonder exactly what effect this stream of relentless innuendo might have on the appeal process, which was about to get under way.

Having met Mr Mignini on several occasions in Perugia, I felt that the accusations being thrown at him were completely unfounded. To me, he comes across as an avuncular man with a pleasant smile, but he is also acutely intelligent, and he appears to be both well liked in the Perugian community and respected by his legal adversaries.

As the accusations and insults were traded in the media, I was becoming increasingly angry at the way that Amanda Knox had been accorded almost minor celebrity status throughout her years in prison. As ever, Raffaele Sollecito had been sidelined by the media and seemed to have been sentenced to anonymity – but the media's appetite for more stories focusing on Amanda Knox seemed to be insatiable. In December 2010, I wrote an article for the *Daily Mail*, in which I said:

> I switched on my television to see the parents of the young woman convicted of taking my daughter's life proclaiming her innocence. And once again I felt the pain and the anger and the raw grief resurface. It seems to me that there is no escape from her or her

jaunty nickname, 'Foxy Knoxy', which I feel trivial-ises things.

Her parents have never expressed their condo-lences to our family for our grievous loss. There has been no letter of sympathy; no word of regret. Instead, I have had to watch them repeatedly reiter-ate the mantra of their daughter's innocence.

Alas, I fear that there is more yet to come. Their TV appearance last week trailed for two days as if it were some exclusive media coup, and coincides with the resumption of Knox's appeal against her convic-tion. This appeal, like the initial court case, will drag on for months, while the dark tunnel between my family and our ability to grieve for Meredith in peace becomes longer.

Yet it is Knox who still exerts such a hold over the media. As a journalist myself, I know the reason why. Knox is young, attractive and female. To many, she seems an unlikely killer.

As a family, our sadness is that our daughter has become 'Meredith Kercher murder victim' and not Meredith Kercher, our lovely, intellectually curious daughter.

I wrote of how her friends leave letters for her at the cemetery and remind her of the times they laughed together. 'None of us, you see, wants to forget her for even one second. So she is here, among us, everywhere. She lives on in the public memorials, with trees planted in her honour, a cherry tree at Old Palace School and an oak at Leeds University.'

There was another memory that will always stick with me:

It was two years after Meredith's death that we were told we could finally take Meredith's possessions home to England with us. I expected a large suitcase full of her belongings, including the opera calendar she kept telling me about on the telephone that she had bought for her mother's birthday, which she was flying home to. We wanted to cherish all of these things. But instead, we were given a small, battered case. Her beloved clothes had all been taken for forensic tests. Not even her treasured possessions were sacrosanct.

During the summer of 2009, while the trial was going on, I had suffered a stroke. I have no real idea what caused it. I'd had several bouts of dizziness that my doctor thought might be attributable to an ear condition, but then, in July, I was hit with the stroke and hospitalised for several days. It was scary and I had double vision for several weeks afterwards but, thankfully, no other complications. I will never know whether the stress of Meredith's death and the subsequent trial affected my health adversely, but it made me question how many more times I could make the trip to Perugia, and how much more of the attendant chaos I was able to bear.

At the same time, and much more happily, Leeds University informed us that they had elected to award

Meredith a posthumous degree in European Politics and Italian. We were so pleased that they had decided to do this, because 2009 was the year that she would have graduated, after having completed a further year in Leeds following her year in Perugia. What delighted us was that her university departments had been campaigning for her award against some hesitation. Meredith, as we had already learned, had touched many people through her university career, and I knew she would have been proud of earning her degree.

Because of my poor health, I was unable to attend the degree ceremony in Leeds, a fact that pained me greatly, as I would have loved to have been there and seen the degree awarded. But, in my absence, Arline, Stephanie, John and Lyle travelled to the university. During the ceremony, it was Stephanie who would collect Meredith's degree on her behalf.

Fortunately, the degree ceremony was shown live on the Internet. At home, I watched on the screen as the degree students filed into the hall and took their seats. Our family was seated at the front of the stage. When Meredith's name was announced, and Stephanie rose to walk on to the platform, there was an incredible reaction from the degree students present. They all rose to their feet and applauded. Even after several minutes, the applause had not disappeared, and it continued as Stephanie walked onstage and collected Meredith's degree for her. Stephanie said afterwards: 'I felt so proud to be able to do this for my sister. She deserved it.'

When they returned home, I went to Arline's house to look at Meredith's certificate and felt so proud. In my mind, I could see her collecting it at the degree ceremony, the photographs of her afterwards in her gown and mortarboard, the celebratory meal we had always enjoyed with our other children. The career that she would have gone on to pursue. I found myself wondering if she might have gone on to become a journalist or gone to work in Brussels as she had once dreamed.

Throughout this time, my family and I greatly anticipated Judge Massei's report detailing exactly why he and the jury had decided to convict Knox and Sollecito and sentence them to twenty-six and twenty-five years respectively. Under Italian law, Massei had up to ninety days after the conviction to present this report, which had to be published publicly. It came in almost to the day, in March 2010. It was an incredible and impressive 400 pages long, and though I could not read it immediately, I waited patiently for a translation to be made by Italian lawyers. Three months later, I was able to immerse myself in it, and it was enlightening.

Judge Massei began by bringing Rudy Guede into the equation. Although Guede was not a part of the main trial, having previously been tried in his own 'fast-track' trial, Massei indicated that the defence lawyers for Knox and Sollecito claimed that Guede was the sole author and perpetrator of Meredith's murder. This was what had become known as 'the lone wolf theory'. Massei indicated that Guede had a soft spot for Knox, and that he was one of the main protagonists in the crime. He backed this up by saying that a handprint on the pillow in Meredith's room was made by Guede, a vaginal swab of the victim contained Guede's DNA, and that his DNA was also found on Meredith's sweatshirt and on the strap of the bra that she was wearing. Guede's DNA was also found on Meredith's purse. Further biological traces were found on toilet paper in the larger bathroom of the cottage, and his footprint, stained with Meredith's blood, was found in the corridor leading to the exit of the house.

Judge Massei moved on to the alleged burglary, which the prosecution claimed had been 'staged'. I found his reasoning quite illuminating. He explained that a few days earlier Guede had broken into a nursery school and had taken with him certain items; in contrast to this, nothing was stolen from the cottage where Meredith and Amanda Knox lived. Judge Massei further pointed out that Guede knew the boys who lived downstairs in the cottage and was acquainted with Meredith and Amanda, so he was unlikely to have broken in and risked being caught by people who knew him.

Regarding this possible 'break-in', Judge Massei explained that, as the shutters to the bedroom window to Romanelli's room had been pulled to, it would have necessitated the burglar having to climb twice up a 3.5 m wall to open them and then return with a rock to smash the window, which he said was highly improbable. To quote, he said: 'This scenario appears totally unlikely, given the effort involved, and the uncertainty of success . . .'

He also pointed to the fact that there were no marks on the wall to indicate that anyone had climbed up to the window. One of the forensic officers, Gioia Brocci, had said: 'We observed both the wall, underneath the window and all of the vegetation underneath the window, and we noted that there were no traces on the wall, no traces of earth, of grass, nothing at all, and none of the vegetation underneath the window appeared to have been trampled. Nothing.'

Judge Massei went on to explain that the rock assumed to have been used to break the window was instead simply placed in Filomena Romanelli's room, that drawers in a dresser had not even been opened, that nothing was taken, and that the glass on top of the clothes scattered in the room suggested that this burglary was simply a simulation.

Massei said that whoever permitted Rudy Guede to enter the house that night was not Meredith, but others who also had the house available and could freely gain access to it.

I knew that Meredith had never spoken to any of our family about Rudy Guede, and her friends also said that she had never mentioned him or been seen with him. As her father, my instinct was that Meredith would never have admitted a stranger into the property, especially when she was alone and had university work to do that evening. She would often telephone me at night when she was walking home to her cottage, because she said that there seemed to be quite a few drug addicts in the area, something that often troubled her. So I would talk to her until she arrived home.

Having explained how Amanda Knox's alibi that she spent the evening of 1 November with Sollecito had no confirmation, Massei said that it was Knox who let Guede into the cottage; Knox, he explained, was the only one with a key, all of the other residents of the cottage being away. He said that Knox, needing to distance herself from every suspicion, had organised the scenario of the broken windowpane and disorder in Romanelli's room with the aim of derailing the investigations. In this, she had been aided by Sollecito.

Judge Massei pointed to inconsistencies in the times that Sollecito claimed to have been on his computer, and also inaccuracies in the time when Amanda said that she and Raffaele had had dinner. Initially, she had said that it was between 9.30 and 10 p.m., and later that it had been at 11 p.m. But Raffaele's father had called his son at 8.42 p.m., a fact corroborated by telephone records. In this call, Raffaele had told his father that he was washing the dishes after dinner. Judge Massei stated: 'Therefore, the statements by Amanda Knox, in which the hour of dinner is postponed until 10 p.m. or 11 p.m., constitute an attempt to reduce, insofar as possible, the length of time devoid of activity that could be documented in some way, during the final hours of 1 November 2007, thus creating an alibi that could put her and Raffaele away from the Via della Pergola house where, precisely during that time, the murder of Meredith Kercher was being perpetrated.'

Having turned his attention to the sightings of Knox and Sollecito by the homeless person Antonio Curatolo, and the times he claimed to have seen them, Judge Massei's report then moved on to Sollecito's computer and mobile-phone activity. According to Judge Massei's report, there was no activity on either of these items until early in the morning of 2 November.

Judge Massei also cited the testimony of the shop owner Marco Quintavalle, who said that he had seen Knox at 7.45 a.m. at his shop, and had given a clear description of her.

The next scenario to be outlined was the fact that Knox and Sollecito had planned a trip for 2 November. In his report, Judge Massei said that Amanda Knox's reasons for returning to the cottage that morning were not credible. In court, Knox had said that she had returned to the cottage to change her clothes and take a shower, but the judge questioned why she had not brought her change of clothes to Sollecito's the previous evening, and why she needed to shower and wash her hair at all, when she had already done both on the evening of 1 November. These, Judge Massei reported, were significant inconsistencies.

Judge Massei then turned to the fact that, when faced with the alleged burglary, Sollecito told police that nothing was missing from Romanelli's room: 'No,' it was claimed he said. 'There has been no theft.'

'It is not understood', the judge said, 'how Raffaele Sollecito could rule out that something (money, jewellery or valuables) that Filomena Romanelli could have kept in any box in her room had not been stolen. It is not understood where he could arrive at the categorical assurance he expressed to the *carabinieri*: "No, there has been no theft."'

The report then questioned an email that Knox sent to friends in America about Meredith's locked door on the morning of 2 November. In this email, Knox claimed that she was the one to discover the locked door. According to the judge: 'Amanda cannot help but give central importance to this locked door and writes, therefore, that this fact induced her to run to the terrace, and to position herself on the window ledge to see if she could see something, and that she was panicking . . . However, when the Postal Police arrived at the cottage, the panic caused by the locked door was not expressed in any way. The issue of Meredith's locked door only occurred when other young people arrived at the house.'

He added: 'The conduct that they both exhibited, consisting of staying away from Meredith's door, in a position which would not allow them to see inside the room, seems explicable only if we admit that Amanda and Raffaele already knew what was beyond the door, and therefore had no reason to look inside the room.'

He stated that the alleged murder weapon, the 31 cm knife found on top of the cutlery in a drawer at Sollecito's apartment, was meticulously stored in a clean and new paper bag, with no other items.

Massei detailed the various blood samples seen and collected by Patrizia Stefanoni, a biologist working with the Forensic Genetics section of the Rome police, particularly in the bathroom, before moving on to the results of the autopsy. This was particularly disturbing for me to read and apparently translators of the report were often in tears. I do not intend to go into details here, but there was a suggestion that Meredith might also have been subjected to strangulation. He also declared that tests showed that Meredith was not intoxicated.

The report outlined Patrizia Stefanoni's testimony to the court on 22 May 2009. It can be a bit complicated, but it is essential to clarify the importance of the DNA evidence. Stefanoni said that:

> . . . with reference to the forensic analysis, DNA analysis can be useful whenever (or if) it is possible to make a comparison. Indeed, the analysis of an unknown specimen alone does not yield the identification of an individual; the technical data thus obtained is only of value if the same technical data is possessed for a given person and one can make the comparison. Thus, if the DNA of a suspect is known, then it is possible to compare that DNA with DNA found in a specimen using the same methodology, with the same analytic means, and state whether the sample does or does not belong to the suspect. Also, the victim of an attack can be compared with a specimen taken from a given place in order to determine whether the specimen leads back to the victim or not.

She went on to say that more than 400 samples were taken for testing and that Meredith's bra was of special importance. 'It had been torn off,' she said. 'The small piece of material with hooks yielded a genetic result showing a mixture of the DNA of the victim and of Raffaele Sollecito.' This, it seemed, was vital in tying Sollecito to the crime. 'Four samples', Stefanoni went on, 'were taken from the sweatshirt. The handbag and the sweatshirt yielded similar results; besides the victim's DNA, the DNA of Rudy Hermann Guede was also found.'

The report also stated that a sample taken from Filomena Romanelli's room yielded 'a mixed genetic profile of the victim and Amanda Knox' and 'the samples taken from the corridor, almost in the middle of the corridor in front of the door to Amanda Knox's room, gave the result: victim plus Knox.'

I found these results in the report interesting because, to my knowledge, these findings did not seem to have been contested by defence lawyers.

The blood samples of mixed genetic profiles that had been found in the bathroom took on some significance when it was stated in the report: 'It should be recalled that Amanda Knox, in the course of her own examination [questioning] had declared that when she had left the house on Via della Pergola on the afternoon of 1 November, the bathroom was clean.'

So how did these mixed-blood genetic profiles come to be? The report said that whoever went into the bathroom and left prints must have been barefoot in Meredith's room.

This court also considers that the components of the mixed trace specimens were deposited simultaneously, and were deposited by Amanda. The mixed trace specimens found in the sink and in the bidet and on the box of cotton buds, therefore, signify that Amanda, soiled with Meredith's blood, entered the bathroom which was right next door to the room in which Meredith had been stabbed. Putting her hand against the door, she left a mark on it, and the dribble of blood which remained is a sign of proof of this, and left a mark also – with Meredith's blood – on the light switch. She touched the cotton bud box which was on the sink, and left a mixed trace specimen of herself and of Meredith. To clean her hands, she used the sink in which, through the act of scrubbing, she left her own biological trace mixed with that of Meredith, and used the bidet, most likely to wash her feet, which must have become bloodstained in Meredith's room, where there were widespread and abundant traces of blood, even on the floor, and where the blood was spattered over various parts of the room. She also left a trace specimen of what appeared to be diluted blood in the bidet, which contained both her own DNA and that of Meredith.

In his closing considerations, having stated that there was no evidence to suggest that Amanda Knox and Raffaele Sollecito had spent the night together at Raffaele's apartment, Judge Massei concluded that they had not spent the evening and night of 1 November together at Sollecito's home uninterruptedly, and without going out until ten thirty the next morning. He said: 'The declarations made on this point by Amanda Knox, and which would have constituted, if they had been true, an alibi for both, were shown to be false, and were aimed therefore at avoiding an investigation into the truth and are therefore considered to be evidence against.'

As his report moved to the inevitability of the convictions, he stated: 'All of the elements put together, and considered singularly, create a comprehensive and complete framework without gaps or incongruities and lead to the inevitable and directly consequential attribution of the crimes to both the accused, for which therefore they have penal responsibility, with the exception of the items listed under Heading D, other than the cellphones, with regard to which no evidence emerged against the accused, who are therefore absolved for the relative residual charge, because it was not proven that the crime was committed.'

Massei then concluded with his sentences of twenty-six years for Knox and twenty-five years for Sollecito.

The judge appeared to me to have comprehensively assembled and assessed all of the evidence to point to the guilt of the accused.

And so it went. As far as my family were concerned, the three people responsible for the murder of our beloved Meredith were serving long sentences that befitted the crime. As we have always said, we did not feel any pleasure in this, only the lingering pain of our loss. As one, the most we could say was that we were satisfied that justice had been done.

Not one of us had the slightest hint of suspicion about the drama that was to unfold in the following year.

As if we, as a family, had not gone through enough, we learned that the American Lifetime television channel was to make a film about Meredith's murder titled *Amanda Knox: Murder on Trial in Italy*.

I was horrified by the prospect of having Meredith's killing turned into entertainment, and shocked to discover that the film-makers had no legal responsibility to us, as the family of the deceased. Meredith, it seemed, could be portrayed without our permission, and perhaps even more upsetting was the idea that she would be portrayed without any thought of doing so accurately by researching what she had been like in life. Just like the rest of the media's reaction to the case, this movie was to be the story of Amanda Knox, in which Meredith's murder was merely a footnote.

Arline told the press: 'I haven't seen the film or the video, but it sounds shocking. I really don't understand how a film can be made when there is an appeal to be heard. It doesn't give the court a fair chance and it also brings this all up again for us, which is always very hard. I said some while ago that I don't understand why it was called *Amanda Knox* when my daughter was the victim.'

The American actress Hayden Panettiere, known for her role in the American television series *Heroes*, had been chosen to play Knox, with unknown British Cambridge graduate Amanda Fernando Stevens to appear as Meredith.

Panettiere said that she would have liked to meet Knox. 'I wish,' she said. 'I know that the Italian Government is being pretty protective of her, as are her lawyers, which is understandable.'

Even Knox's team were displeased at this attempt to turn the judicial process into television entertainment. Knox's lawyer Carlo Dalla Vedova said: 'We have always said that we are not at all happy with this film being made and that we would take action if necessary and we have sent the company a legal warning.'

The film's director, Robert Dornhelm, said: 'Meredith's story is tragic for all those involved. What counts above all is that two mothers have lost their daughters, one in death and the other in jail. What interests me more is the psychology and personality of the protagonists rather than the blood of the crime and the search for those responsible.'

Panettiere said, somewhat naively I thought: 'I'm so privileged to play the role. It's a really great story and a very controversial one. The way that the script is written is well done, in a way that I don't think anyone is going to have a problem with. I'm looking forward to it. I'm really excited about it. It's going to be a really tough project to do, but it will be good.'

What was extremely distressing for me and my family was seeing posted on the Internet still shots from the movie of Meredith screaming and wearing a bra. I telephoned the *Daily Mail* about them, and they confirmed that they would not be running the photos in their paper. Though I appreciated that, a still image from the movie still remains on the Internet, which I find upsetting.

As I said to the *Daily Mail*: 'It's so awful what these film people have done. Your imagination runs riot as it is about what happened but to actually see it like this is very different and very distressing.'

I was offered the chance to see the movie, but I declined as I would never want to be confronted with scenes such as those. My imagination had already run through the final night of Meredith's life so many times, and I did not want to see how a group of film-makers, actors and actresses with no connection to my daughter might have recreated it. There was still so much going on in the real world, without my family having to torture ourselves by subjecting ourselves to the movie, for the appeal processes for Knox, Sollecito and Guede had already begun in earnest, and we had no way of knowing how they were going to unfold.

10

Our Hope for Justice

The Italian judicial system affords people convicted
of crimes two automatic courses of appeal: the first
is to the court that made the original conviction, but
should that appeal be unsuccessful, a final appeal to the
Supreme Court is allowed. With Rudy Guede having
been convicted during his fast-track trial before the trials
of Knox and Sollecito actually began, his would be the
first appeal to be considered.

Before the convictions were handed down to Knox
and Sollecito, Guede's defence team had advanced their
request for an appeal to the court in Perugia. In London,
our family were uncertain about what the outcome of
this would be, but in December 2009 his conviction was
upheld. Even so, his sentence was reduced to twenty-four
years, and because a fast-track trial allows a third of that
sentence to be cut, he was finally sentenced to sixteen
years in jail. This was almost half the sentence he had
originally been handed, a fact that seemed unfair to me
and my family.

Even then, Guede was still protesting his innocence: 'I am not happy,' he stated. 'I'm not guilty.'

Our lawyer, Francesco Maresca, made a statement in which he said that he felt that twenty-four years would have been just, and in keeping with the sentences already given to Knox and Sollecito. For my own part, I did not fully understand the reasoning behind the way in which his sentence had been cut short, and I was not sure what I thought of Guede being imprisoned for sixteen years, while Meredith had had so many years taken from her.

After their first appeal was not successful, Guede's defence team now structured an appeal to the Supreme Court in Rome, which is known as the Court of Cassation. This was the final recourse for Guede and his team; whatever decision or verdict the court came to was final and could not be contested.

As our lawyer explained to us, the Supreme Court does not restage the trial, but instead reviews all the events that have gone before, mostly by closely considering the documentary evidence. The Court of Cassation in Rome is situated in Rome's Hall of Justice and exists to 'ensure the observation and the correct interpretation of the law'. The appeal is heard by a panel of five judges, and the Court of Cassation cannot overrule the trial court's interpretation of the evidence; instead, it can only correct a lower court's interpretation of application of the law, to ensure that lower courts have correctly followed legal procedure. It can be a long process, and in this instance it lasted almost a year, with the result finally being proclaimed in December 2010.

Guede's appeal to the Court of Cassation was presided over by Dr Umberto Giordano and four other judges. When they had made all their deliberations, they issued a report outlining the fact that the first court of appeal had upheld the original guilty verdict for an aggravated crime but reduced the sentence to sixteen years. It then outlined, in some detail, the facts of the discovery of Meredith in her room at the cottage and of the cause of death. It described forensic findings, firstly those not attributable to Guede and then those that were, such as his DNA and his palm print in blood on Meredith's pillowcase. The report said that Rudy Guede's presence in the house had been established beyond reasonable doubt.

Further to this, the report stated that, in the fast-track trial, the court established the fact that Guede's responsibility regarding the crime attributed to him was fully proven. With the events of 1 and 2 November outlined in detail, the report then went on to state that Guede's story that he had known Meredith and that she had invited him for a rendezvous was a falsehood invented by Guede.

Finally, the report stated that the Supreme Court of Cassation rejected the appeal of Guede's defence team. As a result of this, Guede would have to serve his full sixteen years in prison, with no further chance of appeal.

Guede's lawyer, Walter Biscotti, said to the waiting press: 'We are not at all satisfied with this, and we will take this to Strasbourg. We will wait for the motivation and see the best way forward. Rudy is innocent of this crime. We shall never give up and shall continue to go forward.'

Our own lawyer, Mr Maresca, commented: 'One chapter of this story has now closed, and the Kercher family are now waiting for an identical conclusion in the opening appeal of Knox and Sollecito.'

He sounded optimistic.

We would have to wait some time to know the outcome of the appeal launched by the defence teams for Amanda Knox and Raffaele Sollecito, so again my family and I found ourselves in a kind of limbo, with nothing we could do but wait. Naturally, our thoughts were with Meredith – and it was in this period that a student who had studied with Meredith at Leeds University got in touch. In 2007, this student had asked Meredith if she would let him interview her for a project he was working on. She agreed and had a short chat with him, which he recorded. The student let Arline have a copy and she lent it to me. Playing it was both wonderful and sad. It was marvellous to hear Meredith's voice again and the way that she spoke. It was also enlightening to hear her personal views on herself. So here is what she said:

What are you studying and why?
'I'm studying European Studies with Italian, because I'm interested in politics and languages. I became interested in Italian after holidays in the country.'

Did your parents tell you what to study?
'They didn't say "do this" or "do that". My mum was a major influence, because she got me interested in politics by watching the news and various programmes. My father, who is a journalist, was also quite an influence on me, as we shared similar interests like music and books and I liked writing. He taught me to question things.'

How did you find the transition to university?
'The transition was quite easy. I didn't mind going to university. We students are all in the same boat. There are plenty of people that you can talk to and I found it quite easy to make friends. My mum's not well, and I ring her every day to make certain that she is all right and to let her know that I'm fine. I speak to my dad regularly too. Also, I have quite a few friends in and near Leeds, and it's only a few hours by train to go home, if I want to, so that makes it easier.'

What about socialising?
'I get on with everyone I live with and they are around all of the time, so I've got to know them well. I'm quite a social person. We might disagree sometimes, but that's normal. I don't have a huge group of people who go out together. Maybe a few of us . . . and I have a few friends I tell everything to. It's important to have a few close friends. I often open up to people too much and I probably shouldn't. But I like to get perspective on things. You get back from uni sometimes and everyone's there,

so it's nice to go to your own room and reflect on things. I get nervous if I go out on my own at night. But in the daytime I sometimes like to go up to London shopping on my own. You can be yourself. And I quite like getting the train on my own and listening to CDs.'

What do you look for in a relationship?
'Trust. If you're only just getting to know someone, then you need to talk a lot to see what they are like. Never meet someone and you are just getting to know them and think that it might lead to marriage. I don't want to get worried about it. I don't need to depend on someone. So I don't worry whether I am going to meet someone to complete my life.'

Have you found your own identity?
'Difficult to say. Magazines tell you to find "the real you". But in the end, it's what you feel comfortable with, who you are and not pretending to be something you aren't.'

At this stage of events, as we waited to hear any news, it seemed certain that the convictions of Knox and Sollecito would be upheld and we would, at last, get what everyone referred to as 'closure'. As the appeals were prepared and the start of their hearings approached, I reasoned that several different outcomes were possible. At one extreme, the judge could uphold the original convictions and sentences, and open the door for Knox's and Sollecito's defence teams to appeal to the Supreme Court as Guede had done. As a middle ground, he could uphold the convictions but reduce the sentences, in line with how Rudy Guede's appeal had gone, with his sentence being reduced to sixteen years. Finally, at the other extreme, he could overturn the convictions and set both Knox and Sollecito free. Arline and I, discussing this regularly, believed this final course of events to be an unlikely scenario, given just how emphatic the original conviction had been, and the wealth of evidence that the prosecution had presented.

When their appeal process began, our presence as a family was not required in the court in Perugia. Only when the final verdict was to be made would a representation of our family fly out for the result. Between ourselves, we felt that the appeal was simply a process we would have to endure, and that the final result would be the same.

Judge Claudio Pratillo Hellmann, with forty years' legal experience, had been appointed to preside over the appeals, with his assistant judge, Massimi Zanetti, and a six-person jury.

During the main trial, the defence lawyers for Knox and Sollecito had requested that independent experts review the original DNA evidence on the knife allegedly used to kill Meredith, as well as the evidence found on Meredith's bra clasp. This had been denied them. With the appeal process now under way, they reiterated the request – and this time Judge Hellmann granted it. Therefore, two independent DNA experts, Stefano Conti and Carla Vecchiotti from Rome's La Sapienza University, were appointed and given ninety days to run a new set of tests on the DNA samples. There are long pauses in trials of this nature, and the results of their findings were not expected to be presented until the spring of 2011.

Meanwhile, the prosecution had asked for several witnesses to be examined, including a re-examination of the homeless man, Antonio Curatolo, who, during the main trial, claimed to have seen Knox and Sollecito on the night of 1 November 2007, when they claimed to have been at Sollecito's apartment all evening and night.

Defence lawyers were also calling for prisoners Mario Alessi and Luciano Aviello, who were inmates with Rudy Guede, to take the stand.

When they did, the stories that they told the court troubled me greatly – and, from a personal viewpoint, seemed to be ludicrous fabrications.

Alessi was serving life for the kidnapping and killing of an eighteen-month-old baby boy in 2006. Taking the stand, he told the court that Rudy Guede, with whom he was in prison, had told him that Amanda Knox and Raffaele Sollecito were innocent of killing Meredith, and that she had been killed by a friend of Guede's, whom he had not named.

Alessi told the court: 'We were in the exercise yard at the prison and Guede approached me and said that he had something to say. He wanted us to get away from the other inmates and away from the cameras. He said that his appeal was coming up and he didn't know whether to tell the truth or not. He said that the real version of events was different from what had been said on TV.'

However, at this point, Alessi appeared ill and the session was adjourned for two hours.

On his return to the stand, he continued with his testimony. 'Guede asked what benefits he would get if he told the truth. He said that he had met Meredith in a bar with some friends of his. He said that he had followed Meredith home to see where she lived. He returned to the house a few days later with one of his friends, who propositioned her, but Meredith asked them to leave.

'Rudy said that he then went to the bathroom and that, when he came back, the scene was very different. He said that Meredith was on the floor, back down, and that his friend was holding her down by the arms, before they swapped positions.

'Rudy then told me that he had put a small ivory handled knife to her throat and that it had cut her and that his hands were full of blood. He told me that his friend had said: "We need to finish her off or we'll rot in jail . . ."'

Alessi then claimed that Guede told him that his friend had run off, and that Guede had tried to stem the flow of blood from Meredith's wound, before fleeing the scene himself.

Guede, he said, had then met up with his friend, who gave him some cash and told him, 'Now get out of Italy.'

In court, Franceso Maresca showed Alessi a picture of the child for whose murder he was currently serving his sentence, and asked him if he recognised him. Alessi replied in the negative.

Maresca then responded with: 'Well, we all remember him. You are serving a life sentence. We say you are lying.'

To me, nothing in his testimony rang true. When I heard what had transpired in court that day, it seemed to be a melange of confused and fabricated statements. I wondered why Guede would ever have followed Meredith home to see where she lived when he already knew where she was, having visited the boys downstairs at the house on two previous occasions.

Meanwhile, as far as I understood the case, the blade of the small ivory-handled knife that Alessi mentioned would not have matched the large wound on Meredith's neck, or the other two knife wounds she suffered. As had already been established in the main trial, two knives were used in the attack – Alessi's story did not seem to take this into account.

I also wondered why Guede's friend would have offered and given him cash to flee Italy. Nobody had been able to establish what had happened to the money that Meredith had had in her room, which she had withdrawn to pay her rent. If Guede and his 'friend' had both been there when Meredith was murdered, would they not have had this money, enough for Guede to get away?

The next witness on to the stand was a small-time crook, Luciano Aviello, brought to the court from prison to testify about what seemed, to me, an equally, if not more absurd, scenario. On the stand, he said that his brother and a friend were responsible for Meredith's death. He claimed that his brother was being paid a considerable amount of money to steal a valuable painting.

'My family doesn't work, how shall we say, legitimately,' he told the court, 'so it didn't surprise me that he had been asked to do this job. The night of 1 November, I was watching TV and my brother came to the house. The sleeves of his jacket were ripped and he had deep scratches on his arms. There was blood on him. I saw, sticking out of his pocket, a piece of cloth and inside there was a closed flick knife and a set of keys. I asked him to tell me what had happened.'

Aviello said that his brother had entered the house where Meredith lived with the keys. Quickly, he realised that he had gone to the wrong house, for his brother and friends had been confronted by a woman in a dressing gown.

'My brother told me that he had put his hand to her mouth and that she had struggled. He said that he got the knife and stabbed her, before he and his friend had run off.

'There was a wall by the house where I live. I took out a stone and put the keys and knife in there and covered it with earth.'

This story seemed, to me, such an obvious melodramatic fabrication that I could not believe that Knox's and Sollecito's lawyers were basing their appeal on it. When Meredith was found, for instance, she was not wearing a dressing gown. Nor would this 'flick knife' have had a blade compatible with the wounds Meredith sustained. Furthermore, I could not quite understand where the keys with which Aviello's brother was said to have let himself into Meredith's cottage might have come from. As had been established in the main trial, the only two people with keys to the cottage who were in Perugia that night were Amanda Knox and Meredith herself.

If Meredith had caused the scratches on his brother's arms, then there would have been skin tissue under her fingernails, DNA to indicate another person present at her death, other than Guede, Sollecito and Knox – which, of course, was not true. But the final point that made me believe this story was a total fabrication was that it takes no account of Rudy Guede's DNA being on Meredith's body and other locations in her bedroom, or his bloodied palm print on a pillow, or any of the other evidence the prosecution had presented in the main trial to link Knox and Sollecito with having been there.

To me, both these witnesses appeared strange, desperate attempts to throw doubt on the case as already established. I could not understand the logic of the defence teams presenting two separate, contrasting theories – and I also wondered why Aviello's brother had not been tracked down and detained. It seemed that the only people taking this story seriously were Aviello himself and the defence lawyers.

Rudy Guede appeared in court in the June of 2011 to hear a letter being read out, one he had written to the agency News Mediaset in July 2010. In the letter, Guede said that the allegations and stories from Mario Alessi were 'purely and simply the ravings of a sick mind. This fellow is telling lies about things that I never said to him. I never confided in him. I've got nothing to confess and everything that I had to say I've already said to the judges and I'll go on shouting and fighting while I am still alive until the truth itself and justice prevail over such lies.'

Shortly after, Aviello himself requested a meeting with the prosecution and told Manuela Comodi that everything he had said in court was false, that his brother had had nothing to do with Meredith's murder and that his story about the keys and knife had also been untrue. Back home in England, I could not fathom the sense behind his testimony – and wondered what machinations had been going on behind closed doors.

Testifying on behalf of the prosecution were Dr Patrizia Stefanoni, who had conducted the original DNA and forensic testing, and Professor Giuseppe Novelli, a professor of medicine, regarded as the 'father of police forensics'.

Stefanoni had previously appeared at an independent review of the forensic evidence in 2008, during Rudy Guede's fast-track trial. The review was headed by Dr Renato Biondo, head of the DNA unit of the forensic police, and Stefanoni had testified that the original forensic tests were accurate and reliable.

Alberto Intini, head of the Italian police forensic unit, had also said in 2010, when testifying for the prosecution, that the crime scene had not been contaminated.

Our own appointed DNA expert, Professor Francesca

Torricelli, had also testified that she had confirmed Dr Stefanoni's findings.

There was much anticipation from the public – as well, of course, as from my own family – as to what the independent forensic experts, appointed by the court, would conclude. When their report finally came in, they said that the test of Meredith's DNA on the blade of Sollecito's large knife – which had been found at his apartment by police, and which was alleged to be the murder weapon – might have been invalid. Regrettably, they also reported that they could not rule out that there had been no contamination on Meredith's bra clasp, where, according to Stefanoni, Sollecito's DNA had been found.

Stefanoni was furious that the independent experts had criticised her approach and accused her of ignoring international DNA protocols, claiming that they were making basic errors. She challenged the 'accusations', saying: 'I am angry about the false statements in this report. What international protocols are they talking about? The Italian police force is a member of the European Network of Forensic Science Institutes, while they are not.'

Our lawyer, Francesco Maresca, commented that: 'I was surprised that these experts were so certain and gave such strong, drastic opinions, given that they do not have the same number of years of experience under their belt.'

As we digested this difficult information, my family and I began to ask ourselves some very serious questions – and, for the first time, we were incredulous. How had Sollecito's DNA, I wondered, come to be on Meredith's bra clasp, by any means other than him being present at her death? As a number of experts had already testified, contamination would have been impossible, given the protocols they followed – it could not have been transferred from any other place. Furthermore, why were the four freshly mixed blood samples of Knox and Meredith in the cottage not contested by the defence?

It seemed to me everything that had once seemed so certain from so much evidence was now in the balance. The technicalities of the DNA were quite difficult to understand for the layman, so I began to wonder if the jury for the appeal were also finding the scientific technicalities too complex.

Our lawyer got in touch with our family to request our presence in Perugia for the delivery of the appeals trial verdict. Having already been through my stroke, I felt that it would have been too stressful for me to travel, and did not want to risk it. All the same, Arline, Stephanie and Lyle flew out.

At a pre-verdict press conference, Stephanie said: 'It is very difficult to understand what happened that night without knowing the truth. What everyone needs to remember is the brutality of what happened that night, everything that Meredith must have felt that night, everything that she went through, the fear, the terror and not knowing why. She doesn't deserve that; no one deserves that. Meredith has been almost forgotten in all of this.'

Arline said: 'You have to go by the evidence, because there is nothing else. What I want, what they want, doesn't come into it. It is what the police have found, what the science has found, what evidence there is and that's all that you can go on.'

With the case being at the heart of such a vicious media circus, and with politicians having waded into an arena where they surely did not belong, the verdict was going to be shown live on an Internet news channel. At home, far away from my family, I sat in my kitchen with friends, awaiting the moment with an unbearable tension. What had seemed to be a simple procedure when it began now felt so terribly uncertain. The waiting was awful, for I had no idea what the judge was going to say.

On the screen, I could see my family seated in the courtroom, and wished I could have been with them. Then, at last, Judge Hellmann walked into the court and seemed nervous as he made his pronouncement. His words were being translated and the resounding word 'guilty' was heard. Apparently, several newspapers rushed to print the 'guilty' verdict on their websites.

But we had all jumped the gun. The guilty verdict that we had all heard only applied to the wrongful accusation by Knox regarding Patrick Lumumba. She had been found guilty of attempting to pervert the course of justice by falsely accusing an innocent man of Meredith's murder.

Only afterwards did the real bombshell come. Amanda Knox and Raffaele Sollecito, Judge Hellmann pronounced, were acquitted of Meredith's murder. They were being proclaimed innocent, the 'truth' about what had happened to my daughter was evaporating, their convictions were overturned, the sentence quashed – and they were to walk free, as soon as the formalities were concluded.

Hundreds of miles away from the centre of the events, I sat stunned and open-mouthed. Around me, not one of my friends could believe what they had heard. At the most I had thought that perhaps there would be a reduction in Knox's and Sollecito's sentences, or that the convictions from the main trial would be upheld, and a second appeal to the Supreme Court would take place. To hear that they had been acquitted and exonerated of any blame in Meredith's death was staggering.

Arline said: 'I couldn't believe it. When the judge had come into the court, I thought that he had looked strange. And he looked quite old. But the moment that he said that Knox and Sollecito could go free, there was a deafening uproar from outside the court from Italians who had come to hear the verdict.

'When we left through the front entrance with a police escort, we were amazed to see what could have been up to a thousand people of all ages shouting in disgust at the verdict. They didn't like it and were angry.'

Prosecutor Mignini later said: 'Perugia is a quiet town. The fact that people come and cry out "shame" on the ruling, means something.'

The family gave a post-verdict press conference, which I thought was extremely brave of them. It cannot have been easy. Stephanie, replying to questions from the assembled press, said: 'We have said all along that we don't want the wrong people put away for a crime they did not commit. But it's still difficult. We have no answers.'

Lyle responded with: 'While we accept the decision that was handed down and respect the court and the Italian justice system, we do find that we are now left obviously looking at this again and thinking how a decision that was so certain two years ago has been so emphatically overturned now. It feels like we are back to square one.

'Our family has received backing from around the world, including the US, and we are really grateful for the support that we've had. But seeing this case in terms of a UK–US divide is nonsense.'

Arline said: 'When we went to fly home from Perugia airport, at the airport itself total strangers were coming up to us expressing their sorrow and saying that they were ashamed to be Italian.'

In London, Prime Minister David Cameron went on television and, speaking to ITV1's *Daybreak* programme, said: 'I haven't followed every part of this case, but what I would say is that we should be thinking of the family of Meredith Kercher, because those parents, they had an explanation of what happened to their wonderful daughter and that explanation is there no more. Of course, there is still someone there in prison for her murder, but I think that everyone today should be thinking of the family and how they feel.'

Judge Hellmann, speaking afterwards to *La Nazione*, said: 'I'm a little bit tired, but I managed to survive, and that's the important thing. I had an optimum jury and assistant judge [Massimo Zanetti] and we reached the verdict following our conscience. This was a difficult case, controversial, but we did what was in our conscience. I went to bed serene, but I didn't sleep very much. It was a late night. There was too much attention on this case and that was because of the excessive media interest.'

I was stunned when I learned what Judge Hellmann later said about finding Knox and Sollecito not guilty. Speaking to the *Corriere della Sera* newspaper, he explained that his acquittal of Knox and Sollecito was 'the result of the truth that was created in the proceedings. But the real truth may be different. They may be responsible, but the evidence is not there.' In the same interview he went on to say that 'No one has been able to say exactly what happened. The truth will probably remain hidden.' He also said of Rudy Guede: 'I can't say that he is the only one who knows what happened the night of the murder. For sure, he knows, but he isn't going to tell. Maybe the other two who were accused, Amanda Knox and Raffaele Sollecito, know it too.'

This seemed staggering to hear. The very same judge who had freed the two people previously convicted of murdering Meredith seemed to be saying that even though he had watched them walk free, they may well have been guilty. I wondered why, if this was the case, he had not taken a more ambiguous middle ground. Just as Scottish law allows judges there to announce a verdict of 'not proven' for cases where the defendant may well be guilty but the prosecution has not been able to build a strong enough case, the Italians can acquit defendants for 'lack of evidence'. Judge Hellmann's comments after the verdict seemed to imply that this was the rationale behind the decision.

Prosecutor Manuela Comodi, responded with: 'There is no question of a fresh investigation because, as far as we are concerned, Meredith was murdered by Amanda, Raffaele and Rudy Guede.'

I interpreted this as meaning that they would not be reopening the case to look for other suspects. They had done their job and were satisfied with it. As far as the prosecution was concerned, it was only the verdict that had let all of us – the prosecution, my family, Meredith herself – down.

Just as in the original trial, Judge Hellmann was obliged to compile a report, detailing how he, the second judge and the jury had reached their decision. When the report of more than 120 pages was released in December 2011, I found it difficult reading, and found it hard to believe the points of evidence that had been established beyond any doubt, had been overturned. In the report, Hellmann seemed to be saying that all the evidence pointed to only one person being in the house when Meredith had been killed, and that the alleged staged break-in at the cottage was not so, but in fact a real break-in. This flew directly in the face of the report that had been published after the main trial. It brought our family's understanding of what might have happened to Meredith that terrible night back to square one.

I found his assertion that there had not been a simulated break-in astounding. In the main trial report, Judge Massei devoted several pages to analysing why the break-in must have been staged. This involved meticulous detail regarding how an intruder could not have climbed up the wall to Filomena Romanelli's bedroom window, and how, even if he had, he would have had to climb twice, once to open the shutters and the second time to climb with the rock used to smash the window. Massei had also pointed out that the glass from the smashed window lay on top of clothes that had been scattered on the bedroom floor, whereas in a real break-in the glass would have been under the ransacked clothes. Massei also noted that Sollecito had told police that nothing had been taken from the room, when he could not have known that fact until Romanelli returned to the cottage to check. These were all arguments that Hellmann seemed to summarily dismiss.

I wondered how Judge Hellmann had reached the decision that the evidence pointed to only one person being in the house, when Amanda Knox's DNA and blood, mixed with Meredith's, was found in several locations. On top of this, a mixed genetic profile of a bloodied footprint had been found in Romanelli's room. Judge Massei referred to this evidence in his report, but Hellmann did not seem to confront it.

Referring to the witnesses who had appeared in court, Judge Hellmann stated that the prison inmates called by the defence were considered unreliable, as was the homeless man Antonio Curatolo, the implication being that Curatolo's memory was not as good as it used to be. Though I agreed with Hellmann's findings that these witnesses were not to be trusted, it did mean that he seemed to be suggesting that Guede alone was responsible for Meredith's murder. Ever since the terrible day we learned of her death, my family and I have been convinced that more than one person had to have been present to overpower her.

Regarding the murder weapon, Judge Hellmann said that the arguments of defence consultants seemed more convincing than those of the prosecution. He claimed that the bra clasp had been contaminated before it was gathered, and that the clue represented by the presence of Meredith's DNA on the knife could not be considered valid.

To me, this was a remarkable assessment. There had been several forensic and genetic specialists testifying in the main trial, and all of them had claimed that contamination had not taken place. Patrizia Stefanoni had also testified that all the necessary procedures had been correctly followed. She had been extremely annoyed during the appeal trial at suggestions that these procedures had not been followed as they should have been.

The judge then stated: 'The motive of an unplanned choice of evil without purpose by two good youngsters, who were well disposed towards others, is improbable.'

For Judge Hellmann to refer to Knox and Sollecito as 'two good youngsters' sounds more like a defence summing-up, I thought. 'Two youngsters' would have been sufficient.

'It is not up to this court to suggest how the affair [crime] might really have been carried out,' the report went on. 'Nor whether the author of the crime was one or more than one person, nor whether or to what extent other investigative hypotheses might have been neglected.'

Francesco Maresca, speaking to the *Umbria Journal*, said: 'This reasoning leaves us with an even more bitter taste in our mouths, because we consider that the judges gave credence only to the defence-team experts, even on items of evidence of a scientific nature which were never the object of consultation. For them to have completely thrown out the preliminary investigation and the first instance trial seems excessive to me.'

Prosecutor Manuela Comodi said: 'There are no great surprises. It seems to me that there is a lot of room to challenge the sentence. However, that duty lies entirely with the attorney general.'

Stephanie was also astounded at the appeal's verdict, commenting: 'There were originally 10,000 pages of evidence before the main trial. This means that all of that has been overturned.'

Amanda Knox left the court in Perugia crying, and these pictures were beamed all across the world. Once again, the spotlight of the case was being thrown on Amanda Knox, while Raffaele Sollecito quietly slipped away. Of all the news programmes and articles that would be written, not one would pose the real question that should have been central to that day: if Knox and Sollecito did not murder Meredith, then who did? Instead, Amanda Knox would be the star of the show, her return to America seemingly the story that everybody wanted to tell. The very next day, she would be on her way home.

Corrado Maria Daclon, Secretary General of the USA–Italy Foundation, speaking to ABC News of that moment when Knox returned to prison to collect her belongings, said: 'It's difficult to describe the happiness of her fellow prisoners. All of them, 500 to 600, started to greet Amanda from the windows, like soccer stardom, and yelling "Oh, wow, *ciao*. Amanda!" It was really incredible emotion. All the prison was greeting her like a champion. She was so touched, you can't imagine.'

However, what I found strange and intriguing was when Daclon described Knox's return to America. 'The foundation had been working on the plans to get Amanda out of jail for twenty days, carefully studying how to get her out of jail, her arrival in Rome, transfer to the airport, her arrival and transit through a non-public area of the airport.'

He said that the mission had been dubbed 'Return to Freedom'.

They left Perugia by car and were pursued for some distance by paparazzi on motorcycles, but managed to evade and lose them. On their arrival in Rome, Daclon explained: 'Amanda spent the night in a protected place, in the area of Rome. This was not a hotel, as she would have been discovered immediately when she had to hand in her passport.'

The suggestion that they had been planning this for twenty days troubled me greatly, for it seemed to suggest that they might have had advance notice of the acquittal verdict. For months, the media seemed to have been acting as a huge PR machine, repeatedly broadcasting the news that Amanda Knox was coming home – and though I knew it could just have been a contingency plan, I wondered what effect this might have had on the trial.

Before the verdict, our family had met with Francesco Maresca in London. He had seemed apprehensive, more apprehensive than we had ever known him; until that moment, we had always thought of him as having a certain optimism. He had seemed worried about what Judge Hellmann would deliver as a verdict and said to us: 'It's like David fighting Goliath.'

Prosecutor Manuela Comodi had also commented that she had a feeling that Knox and Sollecito might walk free before Christmas.

There had been talk of a private aeroplane waiting to whisk Amanda home, but as it transpired, the day after she was released from prison, she flew on a conventional British Airways flight to Tacoma International Airport. On her arrival, there were many reporters waiting for her, to hear her comments on her freedom. When she met them, she was tearful and holding her hand in front of her, as if she was saying a prayer. She said: 'They are reminding me to speak English because I'm having trouble with that. I'm really overwhelmed, right now . . . I was looking down from the aeroplane and it seemed like everything wasn't real. What's important for me to say is just thank you to everyone who has believed in me, who has defended me, who has supported my family. I just want my family. That's the important thing to me right now. I just want to go and be with them.'

Meanwhile, Raffaele Sollecito seemed to have been completely forgotten amid the media frenzy surrounding Amanda Knox. For four years she had been the focus of attention and Raffaele had been pushed into the background. Even his acquittal and subsequent release from prison had not attracted much attention. On his emergence into the real world, he said of a plastic bracelet he had been wearing: 'It says *Free Amanda and Raffaele.* I have never taken it off since it was given to me. I think that now is the moment to take it off.'

Sollecito's father, Francesco, said: 'It's as if he has been reborn and he is getting used to the simple things in life again, things that he has not been able to do for four years, and this will take some time.'

When he had adjusted to the outside world, Sollecito, now twenty-seven years old, spoke on the Italian TV programme *Quarto Grado*, saying that Amanda Knox had invited him to Seattle. 'I still have a great affection towards her,' he said, 'but nothing else. We were both victims of a cruel injustice and our relationship was overcome by this tragedy. Our lives are linked by circumstance, but now they are very different.'

Of Judge Hellmann's acquittal verdict, he commented: 'The appeal resolved part of the truth, part of what happened, but now the truth needs to be investigated further to find out all of the truth. I, like them' – here he was referring to my own family – 'want justice to uncover what happened. But I don't know what I can do, because I am not a lawyer or an investigator.'

Speaking of his time in prison, he said: 'At the beginning, I had a really hard time. The inmates would threaten and insult me. I was seen as a spoilt brat. They kept saying: "God will punish you . . ." or "You are going down . . ." These were big guys with scarred faces and I was frightened.

'I was in isolation – but then, as time went on, slowly, slowly things started to change and, at the end, when I was released, all of the other inmates were celebrating with me, banging pots and pans on the bars of the cells.'

I am still uncertain if I can adequately put into words what my family's feelings are at this course of events. Naturally, we were stunned to learn of this verdict. It seemed to overturn so much evidence that had previously been presented in court, and the testimonies of so many expert witnesses. When Knox and Sollecito were behind bars, we had felt that we had some form of closure on the case. As we have said, we would never want innocent people to be imprisoned. Yet now we are left thinking: the world cared about justice for Amanda Knox and Raffaele Sollecito, but what about justice for poor Meredith? She was the kindest and most caring person you could imagine, so why was her life taken from her so cruelly? What was the reason? Will we ever know?

The prosecution is now preparing an appeal to the

Supreme Court in Rome. In this instance, they can only appeal on points of law. This appeal, then, will not take the form of a trial, but a review of all the documentary evidence concerned with the case. The court might uphold the acquittal decision. Equally, it might uphold the original convictions. It could even request a retrial. What had once seemed simple will now become complicated again – and now that Amanda Knox is at home in America, the situation may become political again. For if the Supreme Court upholds the convictions of the main trial, it may ask for Amanda Knox to be extradited from America back to Italy. An extradition treaty does exist between the two countries, though at this point in time it has never been implemented.

For my family and me, everything is in limbo. It could be a long time before any final decision is reached – but, perhaps, we will never know the truth.

In the years since she died, I have not had many dreams about Meredith, which is a shame. When I have dreamt of her, she always looks melancholy, and I can do nothing about it; you cannot, after all, control your dreams. But one dream that particularly sticks in my mind is of Meredith standing in front of a microphone in a log cabin. An elderly woman, a music teacher, is conducting her as she sings in the beautiful voice she had. In the dream, I can hear her so clearly. The last line of her song is: 'And I pretend that I'm on a desert island in the rain.' I have always felt that the rain is tears. But I shall never forget that line.

Afterword

I had never heard of the 'white feather' phenomenon until some years ago. The story goes – or so I was told – that when somebody close to you dies, they occasionally send you a white feather to let you know that they are fine and thinking of you. Whether this was true or not, I could have no idea.

In the days after we were allowed to bring Meredith home and bury her, I went to the cemetery alone and, when I returned to my car, a small white feather was fluttering by the driver's door. Soon after, I visited Meredith again – and again I saw a single white feather. After this, it happened on several occasions – but I always thought that it was simply a coincidence.

That was until, sometime later, Stephanie and I were sitting in the garden at a table, and as we talked, a pure white feather floated down and settled between us. I looked up into a clear blue sky. There were no birds. For the first time, I wondered if Meredith really was communicating with us. It was so easy to think that this was a stupid superstition, but I would not stop myself wondering if it was something more.

Then, quite recently, I had a coffee in London with one of Meredith's friends from Perugia, Natalie Hayward. We had been talking generally and about Meredith. When we left and stood outside South Kensington Underground Station, to my amazement a white feather suddenly floated down between Natalie and myself and settled on her hand. I looked up. Once again, the sky was pure blue and there was not a bird in sight.

After Natalie left, I stood at that point for a full ten minutes, looking skywards, and not one bird appeared. Since then, I have heard and read of other people's similar experiences. From this moment on, I like to think that, in some comforting way, Meredith truly is communicating with me. You may think me stupid or superstitious, but it is an experience I have never had before, and for every white feather I see, the feeling grows stronger.

Sometimes other people can say things better than you can yourself, because you are too close to events. This was certainly the case when a complete stranger, a middle-aged American woman whose name we do not know, wrote to us and managed to capture the entire essence of the person Meredith was. Her message, unsolicited but so appreciated, was so poignant that it made us cry. Here is what this American woman wrote about our daughter, which I am proud to publish.

Meredith was an exceptional young woman, who was intelligent, friendly and loving, beginning the adventure of a lifetime. She emerged into the independence of young adulthood with a remarkable ability to make good on all of the advantages that life had given her: a loving family, physical beauty and vitality, intelligence, grace and wit and a desire to excel.

Along with others, I have felt drawn to learn more about this extraordinary young woman, who did everything that she could, it seemed, to be happy, to achieve and to create goodwill among everyone that she encountered. By all accounts, she was conscientious and generous, possessing a grace and sense of responsibility unusual for her age, while retaining a youthful joy and spontaneity.

Over time, I became aware of another, deepening aspect of her story working through me. I thought about how beautifully Meredith moved through the world: her dedication to her studies and focus on future goals; her commitment to family and the value that she placed on all relationships. These were qualities that became a touchstone for me, qualities that I aspired to strengthen in myself. I felt drawn to her radiance as a guiding force for good in my own life.

Most of us will never enjoy, in such abundance, or with such seeming ease, the beauty, joy and success that Meredith possessed and achieved in her short life. But what Meredith knew, what Meredith was, can become a universal lesson. What Meredith, the woman and her life, can teach us, and has certainly taught me, is the value of moving in the world from a place of light and joy. Meredith has set an example, a standard that challenges and inspires us to live in the world differently. Every time that I think of her, I am reminded of this. For those of us who open ourselves to receiving the gift of her radiant beauty, she can serve as a source of inspiration, and a light toward which we can strive.

Upon reading this, I was overwhelmed. I wondered if this lady was clairvoyant, for she had somehow captured the essence of Meredith so perfectly. I could not have written anything better.

It is moments like this that make me believe that it is right that, as a family, we still vow to get justice for our Meredith – who, in death, has somehow changed the lives of so many people, without them having even known her. How these people are so perceptive about her, I do not know, but the fact that she has touched so many unknowns means that, in some way, she still goes on.

Yet the story is far from over. It was not over with the conviction, it was not over with the appeals, and it will not be over for a long time yet. Perhaps it will never be over. The prosecution present at the appeal when the acquittals were granted are now preparing an appeal to the Supreme Court in Rome. In this, they will not be contesting evidential points, but they will be appealing against the way in which the acquittal was reached. The appeal to the Supreme Court is not a trial; instead, it consists of a panel of judges evaluating all of the documentary evidence and the way in which the appeal trial was conducted. In theory, the court could reverse the acquittal and uphold the original convictions – but it is anyone's guess as to the way things will finally turn out.

Whatever the Supreme Court decides will be the finality and closure of the case. Though there has been talk that a retrial of the appeal could be demanded, it seems unlikely that Amanda Knox would return to Italy for it – and I wonder if, once again, politics might invade the process.

Aside from the main case, there are still several subordinate cases to be heard in court. On several occasions, Amanda Knox claimed that she had been 'hit' by police during her original questioning. This has been refuted and contested by up to a dozen police personnel, and because of this they have brought an action against her.

Knox's parents have also been accused of repeating the allegations of her having been 'abused' whilst under questioning, in an interview they gave to *The Times*. Their case will also be heard in court – but whether or not they will attend remains unknown.

Meanwhile, Raffaele Sollecito's family are also to be questioned in court. Firstly, they will be questioned about the video footage – which they obtained legally – of the police discovering Meredith's body, and which was then illegally supplied to the southern Italian television station Telenorba 7, which broadcast pictures of Meredith's body, causing so much anger and distress. As a family, we have also brought a civil case against the television station for this incident.

Sollecito's sister has also been investigated, after a phone tap revealed that she had allegedly tried to pervert the course of justice by trying to influence various political figures to have certain members of the police investigation removed.

We understand that there are to be no more investigations to determine who might have been involved in Meredith's killing. Convinced that they had the people responsible, the prosecution see no grounds for opening a new investigation; this is the avenue they are going to pursue in the appeal to the Supreme Court.

For me and my family, no matter how many court cases follow, no matter how many hearings, no matter how many speeches and investigations, this can never be over. As she was in life, in death Meredith will forever be a part our lives. I recently had one of my rare dreams about her. This time, I woke up not liking what I had seen – for Meredith had appeared to me and sadly told me that she would not be able to return to me, in my dreams, because she was moving on. I was quite distressed by that. Yet sometime later, she did reappear – so, perhaps, she has found a way round whatever it was that was keeping her away. I like to think so – but I want to see her smiling, rather than being melancholy. I want to hear her laugh, which so often dominates my thoughts.

Writing this book about Meredith has meant so much to me. It has not only been about our family's memories of her, but those of her friends, through whom I have learned so much. It has been about experiencing and learning how people around the world, who never even knew her, have been so drawn to her and inspired by her. It has been extremely emotional to hear from them. I know that the population of Italy felt such an affinity with her, because they felt that she looked so much like one of their own. And Italians are so family-oriented that they reached out to us.

As the trial and appeals stretched out over four years, Meredith, for some reason that evades us, seemed to have become almost forgotten. Why this could ever have happened, I still do not understand, for she was the victim of this terrible crime, and the centrepiece of everything that happened on that November night and in the years that followed. The media frenzy that followed the events concentrated almost solely on Amanda Knox, which I found distressing. They delved into every aspect of her life, her personality and her background. Yet the young woman who Meredith was has been overlooked. This book, as I have said, is intended, in some way, to redress the balance and let people around the world know who our daughter and sister was. So many people asked me to write this book, and at first I was reluctant to do so – but the more I listened to them, the more our own memories returned to us, and I wanted to share them with others.

I often look at photographs of Meredith, especially those I have recently rediscovered: of her standing there in her pink ballet outfit; of her performing in school concerts, where I remember her singing and that beautiful voice she had; of the Elizabethan school festival that she took part in; of her sports days; of the holidays that we enjoyed together; of her excited face on Christmas morning, opening her presents, such happy family moments. I see her blowing the candles out on her birthday cakes over the years and her proudly standing in her school uniform. I remember her coming to my home and the dinners that we enjoyed together, the television programmes that we watched and the laughs that we always had.

It is not easy to remember all of this. I still expect that there is going to be a knock on the door, and that I am going to open it and she is going to be standing there. Perhaps this is silly – but I do not think so.

I think about all of the things that we could have experienced, if she had been allowed to have a future. Her work, a marriage, grandchildren; these are things that are never going to be, because someone took it all away from her and from us. It was meaningless. It was more than a tragedy. It was a terrible act, committed by people who could have had no idea how important to the world Meredith was. I think of all the hard work that she put in during her life: her ambitions, the caring attitude that she had for so many people, who are now deprived of it. There are so many people in the world who would have benefited had Meredith been allowed to live, and now they never will.

Her sister Stephanie said: 'No motive was found, because it was difficult to find any reason to hurt her, and it terrifies me to think she might have left us that night, not knowing either. We can only take comfort knowing that she was somewhere that she desperately wanted to be and that she really was enjoying her time there. We still have hope that justice will prevail and, in the darkest of times, the incredible support that has been given to Meredith and us as a family reminds us of why we are still here. We are now working together with friends and colleagues to start a trust fund in Meredith's name to help us with the case and eventually support anyone else who might tragically find themselves in our position, so that her fight might continue and help others. Every 1 November, I shall light a candle for my sister. May she rest in peace.'

So, Meredith, this book is for you, and all of the people who loved you and love you still.

APPENDIX

A List of Prominent People in the Trials

Luca Altieri: Boyfriend of Filomena Romanelli's friend Paola Grande, who was instructed by police to break down Meredith's bedroom door.

Mauro Barbadori: A police officer who testified about the last-known images of Meredith.

Michele Battistelli: A chief inspector in the postal police who first went to the house when Meredith was discovered.

Renato Biondo: Head of the DNA unit of Rome's scientific and forensic police.

Walter Biscotti: Lawyer for Rudy Guede.

Giulia Bongiorno: Prominent Italian lawyer who represented Raffaele Sollecito.

Gioia Brocci: An officer working for the forensic department in Rome who testified for the prosecution as to Amanda Knox's reaction when taken to the house's kitchen.

Marco Brusco: A lawyer for Raffaele Sollecito.

Robyn Butterworth: A friend of Meredith's in Perugia.

Maria Cantwell: Senator for Washington State.

Nara Capezzali: The woman who testified that she heard a terrifying scream, followed by people running on the street, on the night of the murder.

Marco Chiaccheria: Police officer who testified regarding his search of Raffaele Sollecito's house.

Mariano Cingolani: A forensics expert appointed by the judge at the trial.

Aida Colantone: An interpreter employed by the police in Perugia.

Pasqualino Coletta: Driver of the car that broke down outside Meredith's cottage on 1 November 2007.

Manuela Comodi: Co-prosecutor alongside the chief prosecutor, Giuliano Mignini.

Carlo Dalla Vedova: A defence lawyer for Amanda Knox.

Anna Donnino: An interpreter for the Perugian police who testified at the trial about the night of Amanda Knox's questioning.

Gianetta Elisabetta: Daughter of Lana Elisabetta. She testified at the trial about the mobile phones found in her mother's garden.

Lana Elisabetta: The woman who found Meredith's mobile phones in her garden.

Paolo Fazi: Director of the Perugian bank who testified about a withdrawal from Meredith's bank account the day before her murder.

Rita Ficarra: Officer in the Perugian Flying Squad who testified in court that she was present during the questioning of Amanda Knox.

Armando Finzi: A member of the Perugian police

department who found the knife in the kitchen drawer at Sollecito's home.

Alessandra Formica: An Italian woman who told the court that whilst out walking with her boyfriend on the night of the murder, her boyfriend collided with a black man who was running.

Antonio Francaviglia: Fingerprint expert who testified for the prosecution. Only one of Knox's fingerprints was found in the entire house where she lived, and that was on a glass in the kitchen.

Nicodemo Gentile: A lawyer for Rudy Guede.

Luciano Ghirga: A lawyer for Amanda Knox.

Sarah Gino: A DNA expert for the defence.

Eduardo Giobbi: A detective with the Serious Crime Squad in Rome.

Agatino Giunta: Fingerprint expert who testified for the prosecution.

Paola Grande: Friend of Filomena Romanelli and girlfriend of Luca Altieri. She was present when Meredith's body was discovered at the house.

Natalie Hayward: A friend of Meredith's in Perugia who testified at the trial.

Michael Heavey: An American judge who supported Amanda Knox and who requested a change of venue for the trial.

Claudio Pratillo Hellmann: The judge who presided over the appeals of Sollecito and Knox and who ultimately acquitted them of Meredith's murder.

Alberto Intini: Head of the forensic police in Rome.

Amanda Knox: American student from Seattle, originally convicted of Meredith's murder, then acquitted.

Curt Knox: Amanda Knox's biological father.

Luca Lalli: The pathologist who conducted the autopsy on Meredith and who testified at the trial.

Letterio Latella: A cellphone expert who testified for the prosecution.

Diya 'Patrick' Lumumba: Owner of the bar Le Chic, wrongly accused by Amanda Knox of killing Meredith and cleared.

Luca Maori: A lawyer for Raffaele Sollecito.

Francesco Maresca: Our family lawyer from Florence, who brought a parallel civil case against the accused.

Fabio Marzi: A member of the postal police who was at the cottage when Meredith's body was discovered.

Giancarlo Massei: The judge who presided over the main trial and who sentenced Sollecito and Knox.

Claudia Matteini: The judge who presided over the preliminary trial and who sent Knox and Sollecito for the main trial.

Chris Mellas: Husband of Edda Mellas and stepfather of Amanda Knox.

Laura Mezzetti: The young Italian woman who was a flatmate of Meredith, Romanelli and Knox.

Paolo Micheli: Judge at the pretrial.

Giuliano Mignini: Chief prosecutor.

Monica Napoleone: Head of Homicide Squad in the Perugian police, who testified in the trial.

Professor Gianaristade Norelli: Forensic doctor employed as a consultant by our family.

Carlo Pacelli: Patrick Lumumba's lawyer.

Bruno Pallero: A mobile-phone expert who testified at the trial for the defence.

Francesco Pasquali: Testified at the trial for the defence regarding the broken window in Filomena Romanelli's bedroom.

Marco Peria: Police officer in charge of fingerprints results analysis who testified at the trial.

Serena Perna: Lawyer who works with Francesco Maresca and represented our family.

Helen Powell: A friend of Meredith's in Perugia who testified at the trial.

Domenico Giacinto Profazio: An officer with the Perugia Flying Squad who testified at the trial about his search of Meredith's cottage.

Sophie Purton: A friend of Meredith's in Perugia, and the last-known person to have seen her alive after she had walked halfway home with her following dinner with friends.

Marco Quintavalle: Supermarket owner who testified that he saw Amanda Knox early in the morning of 2 November.

Carlo Maria Scotto di Rinaldi: Owner of the shop where Amanda Knox bought sexy underwear soon after Meredith's murder.

Daniela Rocchi: A defence lawyer for Raffaele Sollecito.

Samantha Rodenhurst: A friend of Meredith's in Perugia who testified at the trial.

Filomena Romanelli: Flatmate of Laura Mezzetti, Amanda Knox and Meredith, whose room the prosecution said was the scene of a staged burglary.

Giacomo Silenzi: One of four men who lived in the flat below Meredith and her female flatmates and said to be the boyfriend of Meredith.

Francesco Sollecito: Raffaele Sollecito's father, a prominent urologist from southern Italy.

Vanessa Sollecito: Raffaele Sollecito's sister and a former member of the *carabinieri*.

Patrizia Stefanoni: Highly respected forensics specialist from Rome, with an international reputation, who conducted tests on the knife and Meredith's bra clasp.

Dr Francesca Torricelli: A forensic geneticist, employed by our family, and who testified at the trial.

Acknowledgements

So many people have offered their emotional support to us, and that was invaluable in helping us get through the hard times that we have had since Meredith died. I would like to thank all of them: Meredith's friends throughout her life, who have contributed their memories to this book; her schoolteachers and those who also supported and helped us either directly or indirectly; our lawyer, Francesco Maresca and his team of Serena and Alessandra; the Italian police for their courtesy and help with our travel arrangements, as well as for their vital emotional support. We would also like to thank the Italian people who stuck with us through four years of trauma: the mayor of Perugia; the academic staff at the University for Foreigners in Perugia; the British Consulate in Florence and the British Embassy in Rome for supplying a translator for us on many occasions. And I must not forget all of the people with whom Meredith worked.

Throughout all of this, the True Justice for Meredith Kercher website was a vital resource, and one without which it would have been difficult for us to appreciate fully the case that unfolded around Meredith's murder. For several years the lawyers running the website – without any motivation other than a desire to see true justice done – published daily updates of what was happening in Italy and America. The teams of lawyers in both countries who gave their time for nothing to prepare translations of reports have helped us more than words can say.

I would also like to thank the *Croydon Guardian*, which soon after Meredith's passing set up a tribute site on the Internet, where more than a hundred people contributed messages. Some of these are worth printing here, because it shows what people, many of whom were strangers from all around the world, thought of Meredith. These messages meant, and continue to mean, so much to my family and me.

'Meredith, you were a true gem. I'll never forget you or your gorgeous smile. I'm going to miss you so much, but you'll never be forgotten.'

Ayse, Southampton

'It's a true indication of the type of person that Meredith was, that I hold so many brilliant memories from just a few months. You were a witty, beautiful and special person; an amazing part of that experience. Will miss you painfully, but remember you with a smile on my face.'

Lauren, London

Acknowledgements

'I am so shocked that this tragedy occurred in my own city. Meredith is very much in our thoughts and prayers.'

Angelo, Perugia

'I studied with Meredith for a while, a few years ago, and whilst I didn't know her well, I do know that she was a very special person. She was always happy and kind to everybody that she met. I don't think that I've ever met anyone so nice, but so dedicated. Rest in peace, sweetheart, and may the angels look after you.'

Jaclyn, Leeds

'I never met Meredith, but I'm sad about that. All the population is praying for her.'

Andy, Perugia

'Rest in peace, Meredith. May you suffer no more.'

Jaimie, USA

'Meredith's tragic story has touched so many. What a beautiful young lady. She has been described by many to be someone special.'

Lorri, California

'We will never forget Meredith. Rest in peace.'

Andrea, Brazil

Meredith

'A new, beautiful star has arisen, and now shines in the sky. We'll never forget you, and you will always remain in our hearts.'

Kristal, Rome

'I'm really sorry that Italy wasn't able to protect you. Forgive us, Meredith.'

Lucia, Cagliari, Italy

And a beautiful poem to Meredith from Holland:

Every time I look into her eyes,
I shed a little tear.
Your inner beauty touches my soul,
Knowing you should be here.
And though your path has led you
To walk into the great Mother's arms,
Never will you be forgotten,
Or your wonderful charm.
Life be eternal
We the children bright as light,
Go to your father, king of love,
You are forever in our sight.
Your gentle grace will be missed,
All that was special about you.
May all the love the world contains,
Be yours forevermore true.
Sweet child of beauty, kindness and joy.
Your spirit flies like a dove,
So many need today,

Acknowledgements

And when your smile shone at me,
You showed me again the way.
Be forever in our hearts, and never be blue.

Terry, the Netherlands

When I first read these messages and the others, too many to print here, I cried. And now, reading through them again and typing them up, I am crying again. They show just how much Meredith meant to so many people, and just how much she might have gone on to mean to countless other people, if she had not died on that November night.

People from around the world have written to say how much Meredith has changed their lives. One commented that they had come to realise how important it was to think more about others, something they had not done until reading about Meredith. One woman wrote to say that she had used the name of Meredith as the middle name for her newborn daughter as she wanted the name to live on.

I would like to thank everyone who, along the way, contributed their thoughts and memories so that, even after death, we were able to know more and more about Meredith. I would also like to thank everyone at Hodder, especially Fenella Bates, for helping me to share Meredith's story with the world, Robert Dinsdale, and, of course, Ben Mason of Fox Mason, for all his help in getting the book this far.